HAPPY IS THE DAY

Also by Tom Slack:

Interesting Things About Birds
Thody Bros. — Unusual Window Cleaners

HAPPY IS THE DAY

A SPITFIRE PILOT'S STORY

Tom Slack

New Edition — Including Foreword by
Jeffrey Quill OBE, AFC, FRAeS,
and Comprehensive Index.

UNITED WRITERS
Cornwall

UNITED WRITERS PUBLICATIONS LTD
Ailsa, Castle Gate, Penzance, Cornwall.

British Library Cataloguing in Publication Data

A catalogue record for this book is
available from the British Library.

ISBN 1 85200 048 1

First published 1987
New and revised edition 1993

Copyright (c) 1987 Tom Slack

Printed in Great Britain by
United Writers Publications Ltd
Cornwall

THE AUTHOR
from a charcoal drawing by
the late J. Greenup.

To my three wonderful children,
Marika, Gavin and Alexander who have
caused me so much worry and happiness.

PREFACE

The original notes and illustrations for this book were written and drawn while the author was a prisoner of war in Stalag Luft 3 in Germany. The notes had to omit any information which might have proved useful to the Germans, and they also avoided anything personal which might have embarrassed the author or anyone else at the time.

The story is now complete, with four illustrations redrawn to replace those damaged during the trek through snow from one German Prison Camp to another, ahead of the advancing Russians near the end of the war.

CONTENTS

FOREWORD

by Chief Spitfire Test Pilot
Jeffrey Quill OBE, AFC, FRAeS
President of the Spitfire Society

Tom Slack is known to his many friends — of whom I am proud to be one — as a very active World War II fighter pilot, a keen ornithologist (once on the Council of the Royal Society for the Protection of Birds) and also a rare, unusual and stimulating personality. He had a successful career in commerce before and after the War, and this book recounts his experiences in the RAF, in which he served from 1940 to 1945. The title is taken from an old Service song, of which the chorus is 'Happy is the day when an airman gets his pay'; readers of this book will be left in no doubt that Tom certainly earned his, although he must have cost the RAF a pretty penny in crashed and missing aircraft.

All the main illustrations were drawn by Tom himself and are very light-hearted in character, which is entirely appropriate because life in a Royal Air Force fighter squadron, apart from being very dangerous, was necessarily light-hearted. There was little merit in taking life outwardly seriously, when it was liable to be so short. But fighter pilots took life seriously enough when in the face of the enemy.

In another of Tom's books, a slim volume from the same publisher, titled *Interesting Things About Birds*, Tom refers to one of his favourite birds, the Fulmar, and describes why they remind him so much of his beloved Spitfire. He has developed the attractive fancy that each one of them represents one of the very many Spitfires that were lost in the English Channel (including his own), or in the seas further afield during the war against Hitler's Luftwaffe.

Tom himself is twice a member of the Caterpillar Club, having baled out on two occasions to save his life by parachute, once into German occupied France and once into the sea off Ushant, making him also a member of the RAF Escaping Society and the Goldfish Club.

Jeffrey Quill

Happy is the day
When an airman gets his pay.
(from a humorist's song.)

1

MALAYA

I often used to wonder what forces of fate were at work when I found myself crouching in the shade of a crashed aircraft in the middle of a hostile desert, or dangling helplessly below a swaying parachute, or being interrogated by a suspicious French underground in a pitch-dark crypt, or sitting alone in a fighter dinghy in a choppy sea or on a hard bench in solitary confinement in a German prison, or being imprisoned by the Russians outside Berlin at the end of the war.

Well, it all started when our P & O luxury liner *Ranchi* docked at Singapore in early September 1939, just as the Second World War was declared in Europe. I had been posted by my company to Malaya after enjoying some leave in England, having spent the last two years selling cigarettes for the company in Nigeria.

Life in Malaya was like living in Paradise, especially for a romantic young bachelor. Planters and the commercial community were the equal and often the envy of anyone else, because some were very rich and most were well paid.

One of the attractions of the Far East was the charming and beautiful women, and the way they treated their menfolk. It was impossible not to succumb to their charms, and the stories about them were so numerous it was difficult to know truth from fiction.

There was the famous story of the married Englishman who had told his head boy that his wife was arriving from England that night, but they both forgot to tell the new number two boy who was out on a day off. The next morning, when the latter came to wake up his 'Tuan' with an early morning cup of tea, he saw a naked lady lying beside him so he lifted the mosquito net and gave her a great slap on the bottom. "Wake up Missie," he said, "time to go home."

There is also the story told about me which I am sure is only half true. It is said that I once went over the northern border into Siam, as it was then called, to meet a great friend of mine called Mackenzie who worked for our company in Bangkok. We decided to spend the night in a small hotel in a charming little village on the East Coast, and Mac, who was a serious and very correct individual, thought he should warn me about certain local customs before we arrived.

He said I might find a girl in my room, but I was not to worry because she would agree to leave if asked politely and given a small present. A Siamese boy at the hotel took my suitcase and showed me several rooms, so the story goes, but when the girls weren't absolutely ravishing I would go to the window, overlooking the beautiful palms, golden sands and blue sea, and complain of the view. Finally he showed me to a small room with the most beautiful girl sitting on the end of the bed holding a sweet scented flower on her lap. I went to the window and opened the shutters to find the room faced a brick wall. "You like view?" asked the boy with a faint twinkle in his oriental eyes.

No wonder my father, who spent most of his working life in Siam, had said to me jokingly when I first went abroad that you only needed to learn two things in any foreign language. The first was "Take your clothes off," and the second, "My friend will pay."

Two of my close friends in Malaya, Ian Coullie and Bill Foster, were often to suffer from this second bit of advice, and Bill, with whom I shared a house in Ipoh, even claims that I once gave away his gold fountain pen to a local beauty to save waking him up to borrow some money early one Sunday morning. At another time Ian's fiancée, the lovely Betty, took a long time to forgive him and even longer to forgive me when she saw his car, which he had kindly lent me one night, parked outside a house of ill repute in Kuala Lumpur on her way to work early one morning.

14

When travelling in the north of Malaya I often stayed with Tunku Abdul Rahman who was the District Officer at Kulim in Kedah at the time. He was a great Malay patriot and a bit of a revolutionary firebrand, determined to see that Malaya would one day be governed by Malays and not by the British from Whitehall. At the same time he had a strong affection for the British and for England where he had studied for a degree.

I stayed with him often, which was considered an unusual thing to do in pre-war days. One of his responsibilities was to discourage public performances of cock fighting and fighting fish, which were both traditional sports among Malays, but below his house he had one of the best collections of fighting fish in Kedah.

At night, after a few 'stengahs' of whisky, we would go down to inspect these fish in their glass jars separated from each other by pieces of cardboard. He would let me choose a fish for myself as well as one for him. I removed the pieces of cardboard until I found an aggressive fish for myself, which turned all the colours of the rainbow as it tried to attack the fish in the neighbouring jar. I would then choose a placid looking fish for him and, as he put them together in the fighting jar, we would place bets on our respective champions. I never once won and, after the war, before he had become Malaysia's first Prime Minister, I asked him how I could possibly lose every single time. "My dear boy," he said in his very English accent, "never let a Malay touch your fighting fish, because a little squeeze behind the gills can work wonders."

On a somewhat different note, there was the story about life in the East which helps to explain local values, although this concerned Indonesia and not Malaya. A member of our company in Indonesia had become involved in a homosexual scandal and was hurriedly put on a ship at midnight for England. A replacement was sent from Siam who was a sober, God-fearing Englishman unlikely to get into any mischief. On arrival he reported to the manager who told him about the scandal and gave him firm instructions to leave the company car outside the local brothel every night for the next two weeks to regain the company's good name.

15

Yellow Peril

I travelled all over Malaya, thoroughly enjoying the comfortable life and making lifelong friends like Kim Hong in Kuala Lumpur, Ah Law in Ipoh and Siew Joo in Seremban, but the fact that there was a war in Europe had begun to give me a guilty conscience.

I joined the Royal Artillery Volunteers in Singapore, even qualifying as an Artificer, but I found it deadly dull playing at soldiers in the evenings and at odd weekends. Then the Malayan government decided to finance a scheme for recruiting and training pilots for the RAF as part of its war effort. Selection boards were set up throughout the country, so I left the office secretly one day to apply. I was accepted, subject to a tough medical examination at the RAF base at Seletar which I somehow managed to pass.

I packed my belongings, took leave of my company, and on October 19th, 1940 reported to the newly-formed Government Flying Training School at Singapore's civil airport at Kallang. We were issued with uniforms and huge topees, and we learnt to fly on Tiger Moths painted the bright yellow of RAF training aircraft. On the ground we were taught the secrets of navigation and the theory of flight.

We were given white armbands and the rank of cadet, with all the privileges of officers. A ferocious but admirable RAF Warrant Officer named Griegson was responsible for our discipline on and off the parade ground, and he must have had a heart attack when he saw us for the first time lined up in our ill-fitting uniforms.

There were eleven of us on the course, but only nine passed out as pilots, and of these only five survived the war. Even Warrant Officer Griegson was killed later, leading a bayonet charge against the Japanese. So much for Darwin's theory of the survival of the fittest, because it was usually the bravest and the fittest who were the first to die.

While at Kallang I was called back by my company to report to Freddie Sargant who was our director in London, out on an inspection visit. He ticked me off for resigning, and referred me to a circular letter from the Chairman at home telling everyone to stay at their posts because the war would be won on the economic front and not on the

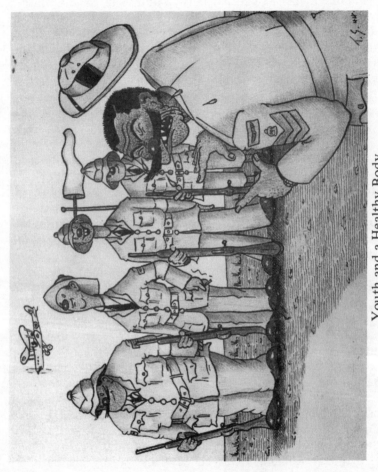

Youth and a Healthy Body

battlefield. When I told him this was unlikely to impress my grandchildren, he jumped up, shook my hand, wished me luck and said he envied me because he had been in the Royal Flying Corps himself in the last war. He told me not to repeat any of this to anyone because he didn't want everyone following suit, but he promised the company would make up my pay for the rest of the war and give me back my job when it was over.

After six weeks training we were due to be attested into the RAF, so the nine of us were paraded on the tarmac at Kallang Airport in front of the Governor and Commander-in-Chief, a quaint old soul named Air Marshall Sir Robert Brooke-Popham. We were then handed over officially to the RAF, who removed our white armbands and 'promoted' us to the humble rank of Leading Aircraftmen, or LACs, with no privileges whatsoever.

After a night's celebration we were taken down to Keppel Harbour in a broken down RAF truck to be put aboard an old cargo ship, bound for Penang, Rangoon and Calcutta. We had a farewell party on board, inviting our instructors from Kallang and friends from Singapore.

I had a great friend on the course called Gordon Lundon, whose parents and sister, named Katie, lived in Singapore and came to the farewell party. I was extremely fond of Katie, although she was engaged to someone else at the time who later died as a prisoner of the Japanese. Gordon and I both played rugger for Singapore on opposite wings and Katie's fiancé was the Captain. When she was watching I seemed to have the extra strength to go like the wind, and a local paper once referred to me as 'twinkle toes Tom'. This took a bit of living down, but it was better than a Nigerian paper's reference to me as a 'ne'er-do-well European sent out to occupy his vacant mind', when a reporter found me trying to teach healthy Africans how to smoke my company's cigarettes in a Lagos back-street.

When Katie left the boat at midnight, just before the ship was due to sail, she pressed a Malayan silver coin into my hand and said it was to bring me luck. Like all pilots I was superstitious so I told her it would worry me to death if I lost it and then what would I do. She stood on tiptoe and kissed my upper lip, telling me that if I left it unshaven it would be a permanent lucky charm. I have a moustache to this day, but it was to cause me problems later when I was trying to escape through France. I also have the coin which turned out to be counterfeit like so many coins in Malaya in those days.

By the end of the war I had collected a whole range of lucky charms. Apart from this counterfeit coin and the moustache, these included a brass 'A' from the lapel of a WAAF officer's uniform, numerous Saint Christopher's, a tiny green frog, and an amazing little metal idol given to me by one of the few gypsies in the WAAF. I don't know what rare metal the idol was made of but it eroded anything it touched, even its own little ring with which it was attached to the other charms. In the end it had to be separated and wrapped in thick greaseproof paper where it has happily survived to this day. Being somewhat of a conservationist, I never flew with a rabbit's foot which was a popular lucky charm for many pilots.

2

EN ROUTE TO HABBANIYA AND IRAQ

When we finally reached Calcutta we travelled across India to Bombay in a dusty old train with no sleeping accommodation or eating facilities. We slept on wooden seats and lived on fruit and chapatti which we bought during the many halts along the route.

Apparently we were not expected in Bombay but the RAF rallied round and billeted us in a half completed transit camp outside the city. From there we were put on board a dirty little tramp steamer, with only hammocks on deck for bunks, for the slow journey up the Persian Gulf to Basra in Iraq, stopping at every primitive port and fishing village en route, long before oil had made this area fabulously rich.

From Basra we travelled north by train to Baghdad, and then by RAF transport for the final stage across the desert to Habbaniya. By now it was early January and freezing cold, and we were surprised to see ice on puddles in the middle of a desert.

Habbaniya was a huge isolated RAF camp, miles from civilization. It lay between the River Euphrates on one side, and a large lake beyond an escarpment on the other. The camp was surrounded by a high perimeter fence of sturdy iron railings with large gates opening onto the desert landing ground and to the one road leading back to civilization.

Habbaniya was the home of the RAF's famous No. 4 Flying Training School which gave initial and advanced training to future fighter and bomber pilots under desert

Accommodation was Arranged

conditions. The fighters flew single-engine Hawker Harts and Audaxes, which were biplanes with fixed undercarriages, and the bombers flew twin engine Oxfords which were monoplanes painted bright yellow.

On arrival we were joined by other pupil pilots from East Africa who had received their Elementary Flying Training in Kenya. Together we were to form the new course at Habbaniya, but first the RAF had to decide who were potential fighter pilots and who were bombers. I would love to know what criteria were used for selection but it seemed that the more happy-go-lucky among us became fighters, and the more serious became bombers, presumably because the latter were considered more responsible. Anyway, I was to be a fighter pilot trained on Harts and Audaxes.

As the camp was so isolated it was designed to be self-sufficient with its own hospital, theatre, NAAFI, library and facilities for playing all the usual British sports including polo and rugger, although the playing fields consisted mostly of stones and sand instead of lush green grass. There was also a sailing club on the lake beyond the escarpment. I even played rugger for Iraq and have a badge and lots of scars to prove it.

In spite of all these amenities it was necessary to escape now and again from the confinement of the camp. So on Sundays we sometimes managed to get away for a drink and a meal at the Airways Rest House on the edge of the lake, where huge Flying Boats used to land on their way to and from the Far East.

The defence of the camp was in the capable hands of the RAF Regiment, with its vintage armoured cars, led by officers of the RAF and supported by a battalion of magnificent Assyrian soldiers.

By the middle of January we were ready to start our training. Our aircraft were housed in hangars facing the exit gates of the perimeter fence, with workshops and lecture rooms behind.

We had to fly dual on Harts to start with but after two and a half hours my instructor jumped out of the rear seat and told me to go solo. After the first solo on Harts we could progress to Audaxes which had no dual controls but space behind the pilot for a rear gunner.

While flying in Singapore we had been taught to pull back the stick on landing when the green turned to grass, but in the desert it was no use waiting until the yellow turned to sand because you would end up six feet under. Another problem with sand and desert was the difficulty of navigation in a plane without radio, once recognisable landmarks had been left behind. There was no question of map reading over an endless desert with shifting sands, and everything depended on accurate compass reading and gauging correctly the speed and direction of any wind. The position of the sun could be of some help in the early morning or late afternoon but not during the middle of the day when it was more or less straight overhead.

In any event, flying these large biplanes was a terrific thrill, and there was something romantic about sitting in an open cockpit with the roar of the powerful engine in front and the wind whistling through the struts and wires of these vintage aircraft.

3

THE SIEGE OF HABBANIYA

At the beginning of April 1941, before we had finished our Initial Flying Training, the British Embassy in Baghdad sent word that there was an Iraqi plot to capture Habbaniya and join forces with Germany and Italy.

Things came to a head when the pro-German Raschid Ali took over the government after a successful coup d'état in Baghdad. Habbaniya was ordered to fly a mass formation over the city to show the flag, hoping this would put the fear of God into Raschid Ali's government and its military leaders.

The camp managed to scrape together fifty-two aircraft, consisting mostly of Harts, Audaxes and Oxfords, with many of them painted training yellow, and on April 9th we took off in mass formation for Baghdad. I was flying an Audax, and it must have been an unbelievable sight for anyone on the ground to see this motley circus of old and odd aircraft rumbling slowly across the desert sky.

If Raschid Ali and his accomplices needed encouragement this was it. Before long they started to move their army across the desert and dig in their troops and artillery along the top of the escarpment overlooking the camp.

At the end of April the Iraqi Commander sent our Commanding Officer an ultimatum to surrender which was rejected. That night we were hurriedly assembled in front of our Commanding Officer who told us we were being prematurely awarded our Flying Badges, or Wings, because we might be required to fly on operations the next day which

25

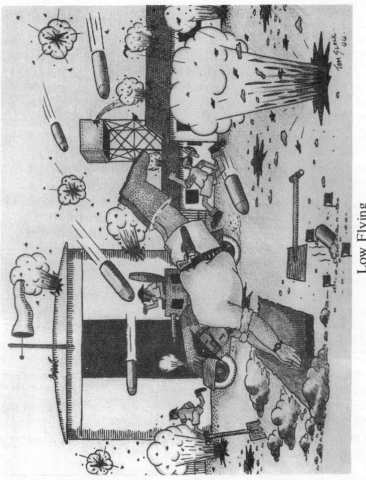

Low Flying

we would have to treat as part of our Advanced Flying Training.

The next morning the fun started. The Iraquis began shelling the camp, while everyone inside worked feverishly to fit bomb racks on the Harts and Audaxes, and rear gun mountings on as many Audaxes as possible. The Oxfords already had bomb racks as part of normal bomber training. Within a very short time No. 4 FTS was ready to take to the air on operations, with instructors and pupils as pilots, and ground crew as rear gunners.

It must have been the first time in RAF history that anything like this had happened, certainly with LACs flying on operations as pilots, because although we had been given our wings someone had forgotten to promote us to Pilot Officers or even to Sergeant Pilots.

In order to bomb or strafe the enemy positions it was necessary to start the aircraft by hand behind the perimeter fence, then taxi at speed through the opened gates turning sharply into the wind to take off at full throttle, while the Iraqis on the escarpment fired at our aircraft with machine guns and artillery over open sights.

Bombing from a Hart or Audax was a hit or miss affair. There was a brass lever on one side of the cockpit which pulled a rod along the underside of the wing to release one large bomb or several smaller ones, and another lever on the other side to release bombs on the other wing. There was no bomb sight so the pilot had to dive at the target and pull up sharply while releasing his bombs. This left only one free hand so it was only possible to release bombs on one wing at a time. This would upset the plane's balance and cause the aircraft to fly crazily until the pilot could regain control.

These aircraft had one gun firing forward, synchronised to fire through the propeller, and if something went wrong the propeller could be peppered with holes. Some Audaxes were fitted with old Vickers 'K' guns at the rear, with bars on the front of the mounting to prevent the gun firing at the pilot and the wings and with other bars at the rear to prevent it firing through the tail. To traverse the gun from one side of the aircraft to the other it had to be lifted manually over the rear bars, which meant it could never

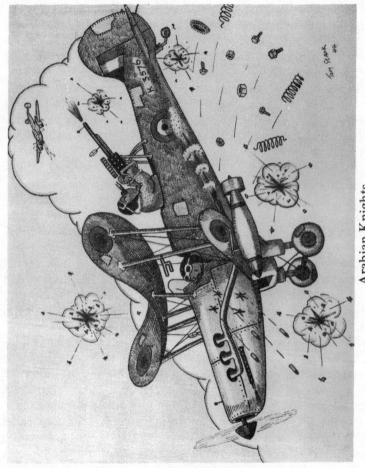

Arabian Knights

be fired at an enemy plane attacking from dead astern.

Besides the training aircraft, there were one or two Gordons and Gladiators, one Blenheim used for reconnaissance, and some Wellingtons which had been flown hurriedly from Egypt to bomb the Iraqi positions. It was obviously dangerous taking off from the main landing ground, with bullets and shells whizzing in all directions and the shells leaving large craters, so the Gladiators and some of the Audaxes started operating from the polo ground in the centre of the camp which was just large enough for them to take off and land.

The Iraqi Air Force appeared from time to time but their bombing was erratic. One of our reconnaissance aircraft spotted their landing ground in the middle of the desert, so a formation was hurriedly sent out which destroyed most of their aircraft on the ground. Raschid Ali then appealed to Germany for help and a few Heinkel IIIs and ME 110s began to appear which caused considerable damage. Even the odd Italian CR 42s flew high over the camp, but the pilots only seemed interested in crazy acrobatics to show off their flying prowess.

The RAF Regiment went out at night to cause havoc among the sleeping enemy. The Assyrian troops were apparently pretty murderous when creeping up on the enemy in the dark, and they gave such a good account of themselves that they have been given permission to wear the RAF shoulder badge on their uniforms.

As the Iraqis were being forced back from the escarpment and away from the vicinity of the camp, it was decided to mount a mass bombing raid on the main aerodrome outside Baghdad. I was flying an Audax which was feeling the effect of the war. The engine was running rough and I was gradually left behind. As I approached Baghdad the main formation and a few stragglers passed me and waved as they headed back for base. I dropped my bombs on the target and was on my way home myself when the engine suddenly spluttered and gave up the ghost. After a quick look round I saw a level piece of desert and made a bumpy forced landing in the middle of Fallujah Plain.

I jumped down from the aircraft and felt in my breast

29

Desert Mouse

pocket to make sure I was carrying my 'Ghoulie Chit'. Some Arabs have been known to mutilate and even castrate their captives, and there were gruesome stories of testicles being sewn in people's mouths before they were released in the scorching desert and told they were free. Hence the name 'Ghoulie Chit' which promised in Kurdish, Turkish and Arabic that anyone delivering the bearer unharmed to any British Post would receive a generous reward.

I had taken the precaution of asking one of the Arab orderlies in the camp to add a postscript to my chit, saying that in my case the reward would be a Prince's ransom.

I had no rear gunner with me on this trip, but the gun was there just in case I had to use it which I hoped would not be the case. We had always been told to stay by our aircraft in an emergency, so I sat under one wing in the shade, waiting for something to happen. I soon felt peckish so I searched the aircraft for the desert rations which were stored for such emergencies. Someone must have scoffed the lot because I couldn't find anything, so the sooner I was rescued the better.

In a short while I saw our aircraft flying overhead in the direction of Baghdad again. I fired my Verey pistol to attract attention and a Gladiator peeled off from the formation and circled overhead to give protection. Gladiators were equipped with radios so the pilot was able to send a message for someone to come from Habbaniya to pick me up.

One of our intrepid instructors called Broughton flew out in an Audax and landed beside my aircraft. He beckoned frantically for me to jump in the back, while he kept his brakes on and the engine racing. He then took off at full throttle, to deliver me safely back at the camp. I reported back to the Squadron Commander, an Australian named Cremin, who gave me a rocket for crash-landing down wind.

Long after the war I took my 'Ghoulie Chit' to Harrods to be translated by one of their Arab interpreters on the fourth floor, because I'd suddenly thought that maybe the orderly had hated my guts and had told anyone capturing me to give me the works. The interpreter turned out to be an Iraqi who confirmed that there was a specially large reward for me, but he appeared to think I was a wanted man and kept asking why I had a price on my head, so I beat a hasty retreat. Anyway, my thanks to that faithful Arab orderly whoever he was and wherever he is today.

By this time units of the British Army and the Arab Legion had made a record dash across the desert from Palestine, first relieving the Fort at Rutbah and then our own besieged camp. They pushed on towards Baghdad while another unit was approaching Baghdad from Basra. The Iraquis had had enough by this time and surrendered. The Prince Regent returned from Egypt where he had been given refuge by the British, and the leaders of the plot were arrested except for Raschid Ali who took refuge in Germany.

Among the many casualties on our side were three from Malaya — Robbie and Blackie were killed, and Ritzie, an American, who had somehow managed to join our British contingent in Singapore, was badly wounded and taken prisoner, but was luckily released when the fighting was over.

Passing through Cairo

4

EGYPT, SOUTHERN AFRICA AND HOME

Six of us, including Gordon from Singapore, were asked to fly some battered Audaxes down to a maintenance unit in Egypt. We didn't have to be asked twice and we took off in loose formation to fly across the desert to the fort at Rutbah where we landed in a sand-storm. An Australian with us overshot the runway, crashing into some boulders, and we had to leave him and his plane at the isolated fort which bore scars of the recent fighting.

It took hours to refuel from four gallon cans before we could fly on to Lydda in Palestine. Navigation was made easy across this last leg of the desert by following the oil pipe-line as far as the Jordan Valley, and after landing at Lydda we were taken by military transport to nearby Tel Aviv. We spent the night and most of our savings in this gay city, before returning to Lydda at dawn for the final leg along the coast over Jaffa, Gaza and the Suez Canal to Egypt. We landed at Gineifa, near the Bitter Lakes, and we were in Egypt at last — the land of the Sphinx, the Pyramids, baksheesh and flies.

We delivered our aircraft to the maintenance unit and were billeted for two weeks in an aircraft hangar at Helwan, where we slept on the floor on straw palliasses. We may have been operational pilots with Wings but we were still humble LACs as far as anyone in the Middle East was concerned. While we were resting on our palliasses we heard on the radio that Hitler had invaded Russia on June 22nd, 1941. Up till then none of us had been quite sure how the war would end, but

African Fauna

35

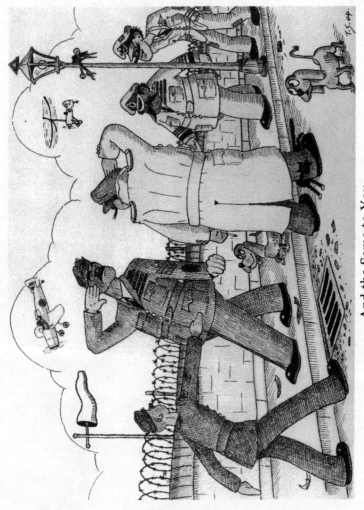

And the Same to You

Hitler must have gone mad and at last we could see the light at the end of the tunnel.

After several visits to Shepherds Hotel and the night clubs in Cairo we boarded an Empire Flying Boat bound for South Africa. The flight took three days, flying more or less office hours from 9 am to 5 pm, and we spent one night in Mozambique, Portuguese East Africa, where we had to wear civilian clothes because our oldest ally was not in the war.

Although it was a flying boat it flew the whole way over land, alighting on rivers and lakes en route. The pilot often flew low so we could see crocodiles lazing on mud flats and all kinds of wild-life, including elephants, feeding on the plains or in the bush.

We finally landed at Vaal Dam, near Johannesburg, where we were taken to spend a week before proceeding north to Rhodesia for further training. In Johannesburg we were treated royally and given the freedom of the exclusive Country Club by a great Anglophile named Jack Ferguson. We were invited to lots of houses and at one of them I fell for a beautiful girl called Elizabeth. When I reached England I used to fly with 'LIZ' on my Spitfire until she wrote to say she had married — a marriage which was to end in tragedy.

From Johannesburg we travelled by rail to Gwelo in Southern Rhodesia to complete our training at the RAF's No. 22 Flying Training School at Thornhill. As we had already flown on operations and had our Wings we were immediately promoted to Sergeant Pilots at long last. We were also told that we were there merely to convert from biplanes to monoplanes which sounded rather impressive.

After seven weeks intensive flying on Harvards, which were nippy little American monoplane trainers, we were commissioned as Pilot Officers and sent our separate ways. Gordon went to South Africa for an advanced navigational course before joining Coastal Command in England, where he was shot down and killed somewhere over the Bay of Biscay. I went with two great friends I had met at Thornhill, Harold Knight from South Africa and Ted Sly from Australia, down to Cape Town to join the good ship *Christiaan Huygens*, bound in a roundabout way for England.

Harold was a tall, dark, shy man with large doleful brown

eyes. His speech was slow and very South African, but he had a quick mind and made a wonderful companion and friend. On the other hand Ted was small, fair and extrovert. He was as bright as a pin with steely blue eyes and a thick Australian accent. Although quite different from Harold, he made an equally valuable friend and the three of us became inseparable.

After a week in Cape Town we sailed due west in the *Christiaan Huygens* to South America and then turned north, hugging the coast past the West Indies and the USA until we docked at St. John, New Brunswick, in Canada. The ship was comfortable enough with a well stocked bar, but the food was terrible so we called ourselves the Hungry Christians. The ship was Dutch, built to ply between Holland and the Dutch East Indies, and it was not capable of withstanding the rough voyage across the Atlantic, so we stayed on board at St. John while the hull was scraped and strengthened.

Like everywhere else, we thoroughly enjoyed ourselves, and Harold, Ted and I were adopted by a marvellous Canadian family called Teed who fed us, washed our clothes, pressed our uniforms, sewed on our buttons and showed us the town. Then came the day in mid-November when we were ready to join a large convoy which was assembling further north for the Atlantic crossing. The weather and visibility were terrible as we steamed north, hugging the coast and picking up other ships along the way before joining the main convoy.

It was a large convoy escorted by a huge fleet of US warships, although America was not in the war at that time. We headed northwards again, to avoid German U-boats, before crossing the Atlantic south of Iceland. The weather became worse and worse each day with snowstorms and raging seas lashing the ships. We took it in turns to relieve the crew on lookout in the crow's nest, although at times we could hardly see beyond our noses, and the pitching and tossing at that height above deck was enough to scare any airman.

Halfway across the Atlantic the US warships turned back after handing the convoy over to two small frigates of the Royal Navy, which saw us safely through mist and fog to Liverpool.

Within twenty-four hours I was home.

Ancestral Home

5

SPITFIRES AND SQUADRON LIFE

After some leave Harold, Ted and I were posted to No. 57 Operational Training Unit at Hawarden, near Chester, to learn to fly Spitfires on battered old Mark IIs which had survived the Battle of Britain.

At first we flew dual and then solo on Miles Masters, to gain experience on monoplanes larger and more powerful than Harvards, and then came the big day when we were led out to a waiting Spitfire. The instructor would explain all the dials and gadgets in the cockpit and warn us what to do, and what not to do, when taking off and landing, including how to counteract torque on take off. He would then get down from the wing and tell us to get airborne. There were no dual controls in Spitfires and it was solo first time.

What a thrill. There has never been a plane like the Spitfire before or since. It looked beautiful and flew beautifully, and I was lucky enough to fly nothing else on operations for the rest of the war, progressing from Spit IIs to IIIs and Vs and finally to XIIs. Unlike most other aircraft, the Spitfire never had to change its name as improved and more powerful versions were introduced, because these were always recognisable as Spitfires. Whereas even the famous Hurricane became a Tempest or a Typhoon, as improved versions appeared bearing little resemblance to the original.

Our instructors were all experienced fighter pilots on rest from operations. They would take us up for mock dog fights, and formation flying in cloud which always seemed to cover northern England. We practised cross country navigation at high and low levels, aerobatics, night flying, firing at air-to-air and air-to-ground targets and how to get out of a spin. On the ground we concentrated on tactics, aircraft recognition and everything about the Spitfire, because the rest had been learnt on former courses.

After nearly four months we were posted to operational squadrons in the south. Harold and I joined 41 Squadron in the Tangmere Wing near Chichester, which was part of Fighter Command's 11 Group, and Ted went to join an Australian Fighter Squadron. Our Squadron crest was the Cross of St. Omer with the motto 'Seek and Destroy', which we were soon to learn should have been 'Seek and be Destroyed'.

The Wing at Tangmere, or Tangers as it was affectionately called, consisted of three fighter squadrons, with one operating from the main aerodrome and two from satellite airfields nearby. 41 Squadron operated from the airfield at Merston which consisted literally of a large field with a few sheds, workshops, small hangars and a dispersal hut for the pilots. I somehow managed to stay with this Squadron from April '42 until I was taken prisoner in August '44, with only one short break wandering through occupied France in the summer of '43.

When we joined the Squadron the Battle of Britain was over and the RAF was on the offensive. Fighter Squadron duties in the south consisted mainly of sweeps, rhubarbs, rangers, escorting bombers over France, weather and shipping reconnaissances, and escorting Air Sea Rescue launches or Naval MTBs in the Channel. Between these activities the Squadron, or one of the flights, would be on immediate thirty minute or one hour readiness, prepared to take off within these time limits. Immediate readiness meant sitting in the aircraft in full flying kit at the end of the runway, ready to take off the moment a Verey pistol was fired from the dispersal hut or control tower, with the instructions coming over the radio after the plane was airborne.

Within a few days of our arrival Harold and I were sent on our first sweep which was over the Boulogne area in France. I see from the entry in my Log Book that the word JESUS

41

Seek and be Destroyed

was written against it, followed by eight exclamation marks and drawings of bursting flak.

We used to sweep the skies of France and the Low Countries to maintain air superiority, and the German fighters would stir like angry bees to sweep us back. They would climb inland and swing round to approach us from above and behind, diving out of the sun to maul any stragglers before diving on at tremendous speed. Both sides would then return to base to lick their wounds and dispute their claims on the dead and the empty sky.

When the weather was unsuitable for sweeps, the Squadron would often be required to operate rhubarbs or rangers, flying twelve, four or just two aircraft. Rhubarbs were low level attacks on specific targets with all the dangers of light flak. Rangers were more popular because pilots were given the choice of target and height, which usually consisted of searching for military transport or railway locomotives and diving down to strafe them with cannon and machine guns.

Shipping reconnaissance could be unpleasant and dangerous. Pilots approached the enemy coast at sea level, to avoid detection by radar, climbing steeply at the last minute to gain height before diving at speed over the first harbour. One wing had to be dipped to be able to see the harbour below, with flak and flaming onions streaking upwards straight at the aircraft. The pilot would then climb out to sea for the dive over the next harbour and so on.

It is difficult to explain adequately the comradeship and excitement of Squadron life on a fighter station in wartime because it was so unique. Fighter Squadrons were small and everyone knew everyone else. We worked closely together and there was great Squadron spirit. There were twenty or so Officer and Sergeant Pilots, who were mostly very young. These were sufficient to fly the maximum of twelve aircraft required if the whole Squadron was airborne, as well as providing reliefs for pilots who were resting or on leave or sick, and to fill the gaps left by those who were killed or missing until replacements arrived. The CO was a Squadron Leader who had two Flight Lieutenants commanding A and B Flights, with ten or so pilots in each Flight.

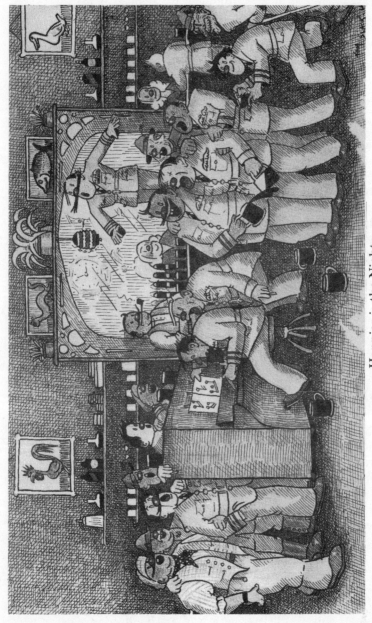

Happier is the Night

When the whole Squadron was airborne the CO would lead a central section of four aircraft, made up of pilots from either or both Flights, and the Flight Commanders would lead sections of four from their own flights on either side of the leader, flying level but slightly behind him.

We had our own Adjutant, Harry Smith, who organised everything and saved us from all sorts of trouble on mornings after, an Engineering Officer called Whippie, a Doctor named Armin and an incredible character named Lord Gisborough, but called Gizzy, who was our Intelligence Officer.

Gizzy was an eccentric and lovable Peer of the Realm from Guisborough, whose spectacles were broken and joined with tape, and who continually puffed at an old pipe which wouldn't draw. He recorded our flying reports on a revolving roll of paper in a battered old leather case with an opening in the front through which he could write. Apparently this contraption was used in the early days of motoring for recording routes which the passenger could follow by turning the paper roll as the journey progressed.

Then there were the dedicated ground staff and ground crews who looked after us and our Spitfires with genuine affection. Last, but in no way least, were the wonderful WAAFs of the Womens' Auxillary Air Force. They drove our transport, cooked and served our food, packed our parachutes, plotted the movements of aircraft in the Operations Room, and made life worth living in many more ways besides.

Officers who were not pilots were sometimes referred to somewhat unkindly as wingless wonders, but only jokingly by the pilots themselves because we would have been lost without them and we were all part of a closely knit and happy team.

Later on, when we were stationed at Hawkinge, it was said that one of their number used to pin a pair of wings on his uniform when going to the cinema in nearby Folkestone where pilots were allowed in free. Worse still, if the show had to be suddenly cancelled, due to a bombing raid or shelling from across the Channel, he would remove the wings and claim the refund offered at the box office on such occasions.

Fighter pilots were permitted, unofficially, to leave the top button of their tunics undone, and sometimes, if we had been flying late, we could be seen in local pubs still wearing our flying boots and those attractive wartime flying jackets. No wonder we were known as Glamour Boys or, less kindly, as Brylcreem Boys, and were usually allowed to get away with murder wherever we went.

I remember one such experience when Harold, Ted and I were learning to fly Spitfires at Hawarden. We had finished our training one day and walked through thick snow and the freezing cold to enjoy ourselves in a local pub. We drank lots of beer and when the pub closed we went outside into the black-out to relieve ourselves against a wall. The local policeman came along and shone his torch towards our faces saying " 'Ullo, 'ullo, what 'ave we 'ere?" As we turned to face him he saw our RAF caps and badges so he switched off his torch and added, "Ah, the Boys in Blue. Carry on lads, and God bless you all." One of our number was unable to discontinue what he had been doing and I dare not think what the policeman must have thought some time later when he found his trouser legs slowly becoming frozen with amber coloured ice, but I am sure he would have forgiven us.

While on leave in London we would often stay at the Turkish Baths in Jermyn Street if we couldn't get a room in a West End hotel. It was cheap, with a lovely hot bath thrown in to clear the cobwebs, and a hot cup of tea with buttered toast first thing in the morning.

One night I couldn't even get a bed in the Baths, so I went to the nearby Cavendish Hotel to try my luck. I had no suitcase, and a somewhat aloof gentleman asked me if I had booked. When I told him I hadn't he informed me politely that there were no vacant rooms. At that moment an elderly lady with white hair came from an office near the entrance and said of course there was a room and told the gentleman to take me upstairs. He led me to an expensive suite and before long he brought me a bottle of champagne in an ice bucket with two glasses. I went downstairs to see the lady to explain that I could hardly afford the room, let alone a bottle of champagne, and could I possibly have a cold beer instead. She smiled and said there were plenty of people in her hotel who wouldn't notice an extra bottle of champagne on their bills and it was the least anyone could do for a young RAF officer. She turned out to be Rosa Lewis, the friend of a king, made nationally famous by the BBC as 'The Duchess of Duke Street'.

In July '42 we were transferred to Debden in East Anglia for a posting to a secret destination. We were issued with tropical kit and, for security reasons, we were all led to understand that we were going to the Middle East, but before very long we were joined by several pilots who had served in Russia, including some who were sporting the Order of Lenin. They told us that our Spitfires were actually on a ship in a convoy bound for Murmansk, and that we would be flown to Russia in RAF transport aircraft as soon as they arrived.

The convoy was the famous PQ 17 which was attacked by the German Navy and suffered crippling losses in the North Sea. Only twelve of the thirty-eight ships in the convoy got through and our Spitfires ended up at the bottom of the sea. Apparently the Admiralty gave the order for the convoy to scatter in the mistaken belief that it was about to be attacked by a large force of German warships including *The Terpitz* — this decision was made against the advice of a young Naval Intelligence Officer who had reason to think otherwise. In fact, *The Terpitz* never left harbour but the Germans were able to pick off the undefended stragglers one by one.

After the war, when this young Naval Intelligence Officer had become Vice-Admiral Sir Norman Denning, he and his wife bought what used to be our family home in Micheldever. I called there once for nostalgic reasons and they were both most kind and hospitable. They had heard in the village that there used to be a deep artesian well at the back somewhere, which supplied water before the days of mains and, having spent years pumping water from 'floor to ceiling', I was able to show them the exact spot.

Anyway our trip to Russia was off, so we returned to the south for a few more weeks of operational flying before the Squadron was posted to Llanbedr in North Wales for a rest.

Joe Birbeck and Peter Cowell joined the Squadron at Llanbedr. Joe had spent some time with the Merchant Shipping Fighter Unit. This was a suicidal outfit which involved sailing in a merchant ship with a Hurricane fighter plane attached to rails on the deck. If the ship was attacked the pilot would jump into the cockpit, start the engine and prepare for take-off. When the engine was at full throttle the crew would ignite rockets which shot the plane over the side at about 70 mph which was just enough to keep it airborne until it could gather speed. Once airborne there was no way back and the pilot either had to bale out over the sea or try to make landfall somewhere. None of this appeared to have worried Joe who ran away from school at the age of sixteen to join up, having altered the date on his birth certificate from 1924 to 1922.

Peter Cowell was equally young and enterprising, and on one shipping reconnaissance carried out at low level in poor visibility, when it was impossible to see the horizon, his Spitfire hit the sea breaking off the ends of the propeller. Somehow he managed to fly back to base to be one of the very few pilots to survive such a frightening experience.

On August 16th, 1942 after less than two weeks rest at Llanbedr, the Squadron was recalled hurriedly to Tangmere for special duties. On the evening of the 18th we received a top secret briefing and everyone was confined to camp with no communication with the outside world. At dawn the next day we took off to cover the Dieppe landings which seemed to go wrong from the start, with the Canadians suffering terrible casualties.

The Squadron made three sorties over Dieppe during the day, most of the time escorting Hurricane bombers at very low level. On one of these our CO crashed in flames at the back of the town and was killed. We were lucky not to lose more pilots since most of our aircraft were hit. There was nothing but flak and confusion over the area, as each side bombed and strafed each other without quite knowing who was where.

Although the operation was considered somewhat of a failure, it at least gave the Canadians the action they had been seeking after spending months in England clicking their heels, and many lessons were learnt which must have stood the Allies in good stead when they finally landed in Europe on 'D' Day.

That night everyone was still very tense so we all trooped

KURDISH

ئەم طيارەجي ئەنگليسيە و ئەوەى كە ناوى ئەنگليسين، ئێستا كە حكومەت عراق ئەستىكار بوەحكومەتا ئەنگليس دەخوازيە بسەر ئەمكار داخلى عراق ئەمەهەرى حكومەي عراقە. ئەو ئەى كارى و مساعدەئ ئەم طيارەجي دەكەن لەطرف حكومەت ئەنگلن تلفيف دەكرێ و ئەمام بانى مەدرئت، ئەما كرام طيارەجي ئاديت بدرێت ئەو ئان كە مسئول دوچار جوازات شديد دمن.

TURKISH

بو طيارە و ئەنگكار طيارەجى در. ئەجنبە ئانگليسين. ئيستا كە حكومەت عراق مستقل اولىندن ركى ئنكانر بو ئان طيارەجىان ئنكاندن روى ئانكانـر حكومى مستقل اولىندن ركى ئانكانـز حكومى عراق داخلـه امورىندن مسئول دكدر. كم بو طيارەجيلرە يارم ايدرسه ئانكاپ حكومى ئرد مكافات و رجىلك فقط اولارە ئانكاپ حكومى خصوصت اولنامى تقدىرودە ئانكانرە حكومى قاصدجى اولا ئلرم ال عمدل كيان قليتش ئيدرومجكا.

ARABIC

ان هذه الطيارة و طيارتها و الذين هم في بريطانيون. منذ ان نال العراق استقلاله أصبحت للحكومة البريطانية مسؤولة عن شؤون العراق الداخلية اذا ذان الطيارة من هذه الشؤون عائدة الان الى الحكومة العراقية وحدها. ان الذين يساعدون كهؤلاء هذه الطيارة ذكسب رضي الحكومة البريطانية التي ستكافؤهم عن خدماتهم بسخاء .. ولكن في حالة اظهار العداء لهم سوف تتخذ اشد التدابير ضد المذنبين.

سمح لي طيارة تخلصوا بنا .. نجدينا انكانا ان انگليزی بسلح حرمنا في البحرين ...

Myself with red scarf and Mae West.

Lord Gisborough — 'Gizzy'.

Another picture of self, 1942.

On readiness outside dispersal hut.
From left: F/Lt Tom Slack, F/o Peter Cowell, 'Perkins',
F/o Barney Newman.

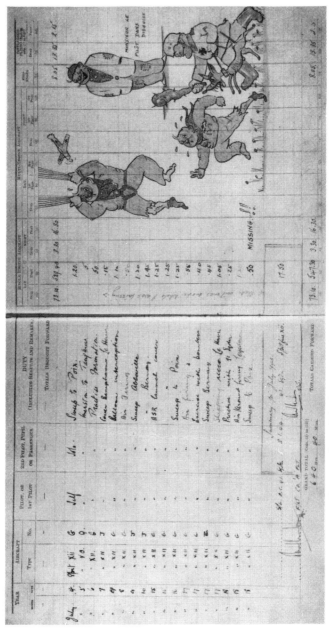

1943 — Extract from Pilot's Log Book. Illustrations unusual and quite unauthorised.

This was a famous wartime photograph of 41 Squadron's Spitfire X11s with clipped wings and Griffon engines. It was used for a popular jigsaw puzzle with EBJ moved slightly back and the plane behind EBH removed altogether to produce a perfect formation.

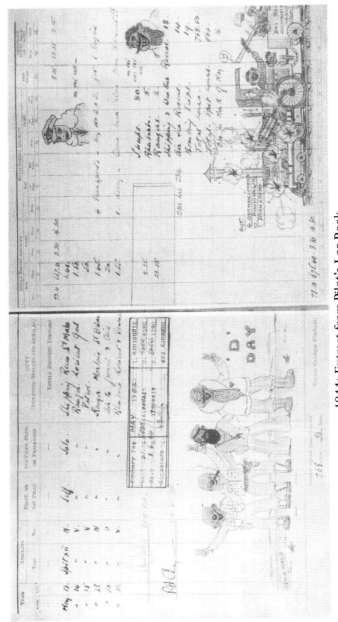

1944: Extract from Pilot's Log Book.

Air Sea Rescue by 276 Sqdn. A/c 'B'. 18th June 1944.

Myself with one Canadian and two American
airmen who came over the Pyrenees together
and were fed and hidden by these ladies in
San Sebastian, North Spain, until whisked
away by our respective embassies.

into Chichester with some WAAF friends to relax and forget our sorrows in the 'Unicorn' and the 'Nag's Head'. Everywhere we went drinks were on the house because Dieppe was the big story of the day. At dawn the next morning we flew back to the peace and quiet of Llanbedr.

Llanbedr was very much in Welsh Wales, where many people still spoke Welsh and there was no drinking in pubs on Sundays, at least officially. A deputation even came from nearby Barmouth to ask us not to fly on the Sabbath.

The small aerodrome lay between the little village and the sand dunes near the sea, not far from the ruins of Harlech Castle. While there I became very friendly with a poacher who taught me how to fish by tickling trout. One day he asked me back to his cottage to meet his wife and have some tea. We sat there waiting for her and when she failed to appear he went to the kitchen to find out what was wrong. He returned to say he was sorry but she didn't want to meet me because she could never forgive what happened up at the Castle. Members of the Squadron sometimes went to Harlech for a night out so I asked him what on earth we had done wrong. It was nothing to do with the RAF or the Squadron he told me, but with the English who had sacked the Castle in the fifteenth century. As I have said, Llanbedr was very much in Welsh Wales.

Although we were there for a rest, we lost four pilots either flying into the mountains in bad weather or crashing while firing at ground targets. Harold left the Squadron while we were there to join another fighter Squadron in the south where he was eventually killed on operations over France.

Now and again the Squadron would return south for a few days to carry out sweeps and rhubarbs to brush away the cobwebs. But apart from this we just practised formation and night flying, high and low level navigation across country, and firing at air to ground targets. The only real excitement was when we were sometimes scrambled to intercept JU88s flying low over the Irish Sea, but we never caught one.

In January 1943 I was sent on the Fighter Leaders' Course at Chedworth, which was run by some of the most famous pilots in Fighter Command, like Laddy Lucas and Brian

c

Scramble at Dawn

Kingcome. The main purpose of the course was to experiment with different tactics for aerial combat, but the weather was terrible and we only got in a few hours flying. It was just as well because the Spits were Mark IIs, like the ones at Hawarden but that much older, and they were just about on their last legs.

On the final day we were visited by Air Chief Marshal Sir Trafford Leigh Mallory who had a long chat with each of us in turn. He must have done his homework because he knew about all of us and our Squadrons without any prompting from anyone.

After a short spell back at Llanbedr the Squadron was posted at the end of February 1943 to High Ercall in Shropshire to be equipped with the latest secret Spitfire. It turned out to be the Spit XII, with a huge powerful Griffon engine to replace the famous Merlin. It had clipped wings for high speed at low level and a high pointed tail, instead of the normal rounded one, to help counteract vicious torque on take-off.

After a month of indoctrination we moved to Hawkinge, near Folkestone, and then on to Friston on the top of Beachy Head, to intercept the low level tip and run raiders which were dropping bombs on towns along the south coast. They used to cross the coast at sea level at places like Birling Gap, to avoid detection by radar, so the Squadron had to be on constant patrol or readiness from dawn to dusk.

Finally at the end of June we were posted back to good old Tangmere, operating this time from the airfield at Westhampnett, to continue the usual routine operations over France and the Channel.

While at Westhampnett Joe Birbeck and I flew together in a Tiger Moth to act as ushers at the wedding of Joan im Thurn and Gerald Nabarro in Winchester Cathedral. The im Thurns were a well known Winchester family and Joan's father, a proud old Colonel, was worried that although his daughter was in the services her future husband was not. He wanted to ensure a military flavour at the wedding so we were able to give him and the guests a wonderful surprise by arranging for four Spitfires from the Squadron to dip in salute over the wedding reception in the gardens of the lovely im Thurn's home.

6

A CONTINENTAL HOLIDAY

In the early afternoon of July 18th, 1943, the Wing was briefed for a sweep over the Poix and Abbeville area of France. It was a lovely summer day with a thin layer of cirrus cloud almost covering the sky.

We were in great spirits on the way to our dispersal huts because we were flying the latest type of Spitfire and were due to sweep at its best operational height of 15,000 feet, with the other two Squadrons stepped up above and behind us for protection. We had approached Poix without incident, when about a dozen yellow-nosed Messerschmitts suddenly appeared out of the sun just behind and above us. They were from the famous Goering Squadron. We must have spotted each other at the same time because two of them rolled over into a dive with our Wing Commander from above in hot pursuit. Another flew over the top of us so I pulled up to get in a quick burst of fire.

Before I could press the firing button a series of explosions shook my aircraft. In the excitement I had forgotten to watch my tail and another Messerschmitt was firing at me from dead astern. By this time I was separated from the Squadron so I skidded and weaved all over the sky to make the German's aim more difficult. I was gradually losing height, and when smoke or glycol started pouring from the engine, I ripped off my helmet, released the safety straps, turned the aircraft onto its back and tried to bale out. My parachute got caught in the cockpit hood so I started to kick frantically. My foot must have pushed the stick forward because I was

Continental Holiday

suddenly thrown clear to tumble head over heels towards France and a continental holiday.

After the roar of the engine and the rushing slipstream everything was now deadly quiet as I pulled the ripcord. White silk streamed out above me and then it opened, pulling me up with a jolt. As I swung in the harness a Messerschmitt circled around and then flew straight at me, pulling up at the last minute to collapse my parachute in its slipstream for a few frightening seconds. However, the pilot was sporting enough not to open fire and I landed with a bump in a cornfield near Abbeville.

Before I could disentangle myself from my parachute two Frenchmen from a group working in the field grabbed my arms and appeared to be arresting me. When the Messerschmitt pilot saw this he waggled his wings, waved from the cockpit and flew away. The Frenchmen gave me the 'V' for victory sign and a push, pointing to nearby woods, and I was off as fast as my shaking legs would carry me. I entered the woods and headed south east, trying to cover as much ground as quickly as possible between me and the cornfield, in case the Germans decided to mount a search with their tracker dogs.

I had left the far side of the woods and was creeping along a ditch when a sheepdog disclosed my presence to a shepherd. He stood on the bank and eyed me suspiciously, asking what on earth I was doing crawling around in the dirt. I told him I was trying to get back to England. This proved too much for him and we both collapsed with laughter.

He led me into some other woods across several fields where there was a small deserted hut. He told me to stay there while he went to fetch something to eat and drink. We always flew with an oilskin envelope containing an escape kit so while I was waiting I decided to see what it contained. There was a silk map of France, some French currency, and four passport photographs of me taken at Tangmere with a flowing moustache, a black RAF tie and an old sports coat which must have been used for all such photographs taken at the station. There was also a piece of black thread with a magnetic button on the end which had a fluorescent

What do we do Now?

dot pointing to North, a short fishing line with a rubber worm on a hook, some bars of concentrated chocolate and several Benzedrine tablets.

Also the top brass button of our uniforms was designed to unscrew to expose an additional compass, but I was flying in battle dress with no such buttons. There is the story that when the Germans discovered this compass on some prisoners the RAF Intelligence changed the thread from right to left which fooled the Germans for the rest of the war.

Before long the shepherd returned with some bread and warm milk, which I devoured eagerly. However, he appeared very nervous and, although obviously wanting to help, I could see there was nothing more he could do, so I thanked him profusely and carried on into the dusk. It was getting cold so I curled up inside a stook of wheat on the edge of a cornfield and tried to get some sleep, but I had misguidedly taken a Benzedrine tablet after leaving the shepherd which kept me bright-eyed and wide awake for most of the night.

At dawn I continued my travels, keeping to woods and hedgerows until I spotted an isolated small farmhouse in a clearing. I watched it for some time and, as there was no movement, I decided I would risk knocking at the back door. A pleasant looking farmer answered the door in his night clothes. He looked me up and down suspiciously but after a few questions he beckoned for me to come quickly inside into a large untidy room where his wife and daughter were still in bed. His wife lay there fast asleep but his lovely daughter was sitting up to see what on earth was going on.

They bombarded me with questions about life in England, the date of the second front, how long the war would last and who would win. This soon woke up the farmer's wife and she and the daughter dabbed a cut on my leg with disinfectant, sewed up a tear in my trousers, and gave me something to eat and drink. When they had finished the farmer told me he was nervous in case someone had seen me and the Germans decided to organise a search. After filling my pockets with more food and drink they wished me luck and I wandered back into the woods to continue

56

Love at First Light

my journey through unhappy France.

I still had a few Benzedrine tablets to keep me going without a break until evening, but then I was exhausted and made myself comfortable behind a fallen tree trunk near a woodland path.

Suddenly there was the sound of a bicycle rattling along the path and I peered cautiously over the trunk to see a Frenchman approaching, humming away happily to himself. He must have seen me because his humming stopped as he continued slowly down the path. After a short distance he stopped, dismounted and walked back to peer at me suspiciously. When he saw my wings and battledress and after I had confirmed I was a pilot in the RAF, trying to get back to England, he leaped over the tree-trunk, threw his arms round me and started kissing me on both cheeks, which was a new and embarrassing experience for an Englishman.

He told me to remain hidden while he went to the village for some food, drink and civilian clothes and, with a wave, he shot off at speed down the bumpy path. He returned shortly with four companions, two men and two women, who were carrying clothes, food and wine. They gave me a little black beret, a dusty old brown coat, some canvas shoes and a pair of blue trousers, so I disappeared into the bushes to emerge looking like a true French peasant, except for the RAF moustache.

We all sat down to eat the food and wash it down with quantities of good red wine. My original friend insisted on toasting everything and everybody including the RAF, Churchill, Roosevelt, De Gaulle and the Free French, Stalin and Chiang Kai-shek. The birds in their roosts were becoming disturbed by all the noise and excitement, so my friend decided to take me down to the village under the cover of darkness. He led me to a small shed at the bottom of somebody's garden, where I lay on a pile of straw and fell fast asleep.

The Germans had a habit of masquerading as Allied pilots to infiltrate the French underground and discover the escape routes. Anyone helping them would eventually be rounded up and sent to a Concentration Camp or shot. My friends were taking no chances so they sent for an Irishman named

Joseph Balfe, who was a naturalised Frenchman married to a French lady who ran a small café in the nearby village of Hornoy. He arrived on a bicycle early the next morning to ply me with all sorts of questions to check my identity. He was soon satisfied that I was genuine and offered to hide me in his café.

However, everyone insisted that I would first have to shave off my moustache because no Frenchman would be seen dead in occupied France with a typical Englishman sporting an RAF moustache, no matter what clothes he was wearing. I explained that this was impossible, and told them about Katie kissing my upper lip on a cargo boat in Singapore to bring me luck if I left it unshaven.

This was too much for Joseph and his friends who huddled in a corner to discuss this ridiculous development. They soon came up with a compromise and asked if I would agree to have the moustache cut with scissors, which would still leave short stubble on the upper lip. Of course I agreed, and after they had clipped my moustache, they lent me a bicycle and I set off for Hornoy with Joseph, riding some distance behind him so that he could disown me in case of trouble. No one took any notice of me so perhaps I was beginning to look like a real French peasant after all.

7

STAYING WITH FRIENDS

I stayed with Joseph Balfe's family for a week, hidden at the back of their house behind the café which supplied me with delicious food in spite of the severe rationing. Joseph had been in the Irish Guards in France during the First World War and, apart from falling in love and marrying a French girl, he had also won the coveted Military Medal. There was a photograph of him in uniform wearing the medal on the wall of the café, in spite of the fact that German soldiers came to eat and drink there every night.

One day there was a rumour that the Germans were about to make a house to house search in the village because a suspicious character had been seen wandering about in the vicinity. As they started searching at one end of the village, people with guilty consciences began trickling out of the other. Joseph decided it was time I left, and one of his sons, also called Joseph, led me across some fields to a small railway station where we took a crowded train to Amiens.

There were several German soldiers on the train, but again no one took the slightest notice of me. The black beret and my humble clothes were certainly proving to be a good disguise and the only remaining problem was the signet ring on my little finger. I had to remember to turn the crest inwards so that it looked like a wedding ring. It was impossible to take it off because a Nigerian goldsmith had shrunk it onto my finger after I had lost the original one in the surf on Victoria Beach near Lagos.

When I said good-bye to Joseph Senior at the café, I wanted

Morning Tub

to give him something to show my appreciation because he was such a brave and wonderful character and had risked so much. The only thing I had on me was a silver snuffbox given to my father in Siam which he had given to me. It was the type which you squeezed at each end to pop the lid open and I used it as a tobacco pouch for my pipe. I gave it to Joseph who at first refused, but he finally accepted with a promise that after the war he would somehow get it back to me. He kept his promise.

The train journey to Amiens was uneventful, and I was relieved to see that it was a lovely summer's day with a cloudless sky, because I would have hated to meet up with members of our Squadron out on a ranger, diving out of the clouds to shoot up every locomotive and train in sight. When we arrived in Amiens I was distressed to see the enormous damage it had suffered in the war.

Joseph's son took me to a small hairdresser's shop near the station which was owned by Jean Le Mattre. We sat on chairs as though waiting for a haircut, while Jean and his beautiful assistant kept snipping away with their scissors. When they had finished their last customer Jean locked the door, closed the shutters and rushed over to greet us.

Joseph's son had to return to Hornoy before dark, but before he left he asked me to tell the authorities in England that he wanted to escape to join the Forces and could someone please help him to do so. This I did when I arrived back and one day he telephoned me at the Squadron to say he was in London so I rushed up to see him and celebrate. He joined the British Army rather than the Free French and after the war settled in East Anglia.

Jean Le Mattre hid me in an attic in his house behind the shop for nearly a week. He was an ardent De Gaullist, Saboteur and Franc Tireur. In the evenings I used to meet his incredible friends who told gory stories about killing Germans at night and derailing trains by day.

The method they said they used for derailing trains sounded simple but effective. They scraped the gravel and earth from underneath the rail on one side of the line and then repeated this on alternate sides at carefully spaced intervals. The locomotive would dip to one side and then to the other, rolling from side to side with increasing momentum until it leapt the rails followed by the carriages or wagons behind it.

One of our elderly visitors was a French pilot from the First World War who owned a garage and workshop nearby. He ran a clandestine printing press and supplied me with the most beautifully forged papers and documents to see me safely through France.

With true Gallic wit my papers claimed I was a barber at St. Omer aerodrome and I had a special pass, signed and stamped by the Commanding Officer, to allow me to visit my mother who was desperately ill near the Spanish border. The only problem was that some of these documents had to have photographs attached, embossed with an official stamp. Mine of course showed me in a British sports jacket with flowing moustache, so Jean and the forger had to risk taking me to a studio to have new photographs taken. When I got back to England, I mentioned this problem to RAF Intelligence and also at every RAF station I visited on a lecture tour, but I had no luck, and pilots with handle-bar moustaches continued to fly with unsuitable escape photographs throughout the war.

One morning an intrepid lady visited us and offered to take me over the border into Switzerland. I declined politely because it would only have meant escaping from Switzerland back through France again to reach England.

The mention of Switzerland reminds me of a Swiss in our company who was sent to manage our branch in Malta to give him wider experience before promotion to higher things. When asked how he was enjoying life he said everything was fine except for some of our strange English customs, particularly the one where we allowed women to go first through doors. Apparently this was unheard of in democratic Switzerland, where women hadn't even been given the right to vote at the time, and he was worried that his wife might not accept the Swiss way of life when they returned home. However, when it was explained that this custom went back to the dark ages, when people lived in caves and women were made to enter first in case there was a sabre-toothed tiger or some other wild animal lurking in the shadows, his face lit up and from then onwards he was happy to let his wife go first through every door in sight.

It was just as well I turned down the offer of escaping via Switzerland because Jean was soon put in touch with people in Paris who ran an organised escape route down to Southern France and over the Pyrenees.

I was put on a train to Paris equipped with my full set of papers and documents. I was told I would be met by someone carrying a red book who would give me a ticket for the métro, or underground, and I was to follow this person at a safe distance. This was to happen throughout Paris where it was always a red book to follow, or a blue one or an umbrella or something, and always at a safe distance without being allowed to talk to the person or know who they were.

Waiting at the station in Paris was a lady carrying the red book who brushed past me to put the métro ticket in my hand. I followed her down into the métro and onto a train, which was an alarming experience for anyone who had never travelled on the Paris underground before. When she got out I followed her out of the station where no one took my ticket so I still have it to this day.

She led me to a Catholic Church, where she knelt and crossed herself. I made an effort to follow suit but I was not sure how to do it as she had her back to me. Then she led me down to a dark crypt where I could discern dark forms standing in the shadows. A man's voice started to ask me some searching questions. I was obviously now in the hands of a really professional escape organisation which was taking no chances.

I was asked what was meant by initials like PT, PTO, ETA and NBG. I had no difficulty with these so I was then asked what was meant by the word 'blackouts'. I explained about blacking out windows and lights at night so that bombers wouldn't know the difference between a town and open country, and also about pilots blacking out in a tight turn. However, my interrogator didn't seem satisfied and told me to go on. I couldn't believe it but I asked if he was possibly thinking of the word sometimes used in the RAF when referring to a WAAF's dark service knickers. At this the crypt rang out with unsaintly laughter, and I was told I had passed the test with flying colours.

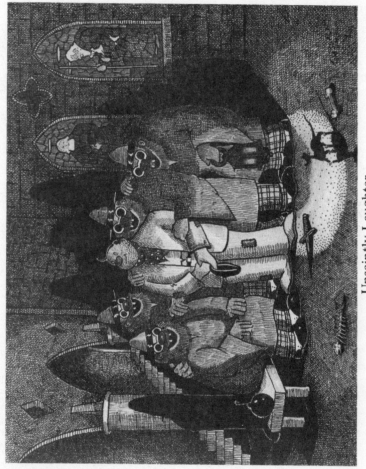

Unsaintly Laughter

I was told to follow my guide again who led me to a flat somewhere in the suburbs of Paris occupied by a pleasant, middle aged couple. They were so excited to have a RAF pilot in their home that they invited several neighbours in for a drink. After a few glasses of wine everyone was informed proudly, with a knowing wink, that I was a 'petit oiseau' who had dropped out of the sky to pay France a fleeting visit. Before long everyone guessed I was either a spy or an airman, and someone must have told the escape organisation because, before dawn the next morning, I was whisked away to the other side of Paris.

There I stayed three nights with a charming gentleman from Alsace-Lorraine who said his name was Hausherr. He was cultured and courteous and must have seen better times, although in Paris he was scraping a living as a tailor. He had an attractive niece who used to visit him during the day to cook a hot meal for the two of us. He made me sleep in his bed, while he moved to a tiny room nearby, and he lent me his night shirt, night cap and bed socks to sleep in. This is a custom I have treasured ever since because it is almost a guarantee against catching the common cold.

One room overlooked the roof of a huge factory with anti-aircraft gun emplacements at each corner, surrounded by sandbags and manned by Germans twenty-four hours a day. It seemed strange to be looking at Germans at such close quarters and yet feel perfectly safe.

After the war I told the RAF Escaping Society about M. Hausherr but he had vanished without trace. I hope he is back home somewhere in Alsace-Lorraine, living like a Lord under his proper name.

8

OVER THE PYRENEES TO GIBRALTAR AND HOME

Early in the morning on the fourth day a mysterious character came to see M. Hausherr who told me the time had come for me to be taken south across the Pyrenees.

I was given a railway ticket to Dax, near Bayonne, not far from the Spanish border, and I was told a guide was waiting across the road to lead me to the main railway station for the south. On arrival at the station another guide, carrying a blue book, would lead me to the right platform, and when he got on the train I was to enter the next compartment.

We arrived early but my compartment was already packed with Frenchmen, talking excitedly, and there was also a solemn looking German soldier who they all ignored.

Looking out of the window I noticed some other strange people who I could have sworn were Americans in disguise. I had heard the story going round Paris that there were so many Americans passing through that you couldn't get a room or a girl anywhere.

After the train had left Paris one of the Frenchmen tried to engage me in conversation, but I feigned deafness and pretended to sleep or read a French newspaper for the rest of the journey. I remembered to turn my signet ring inwards but I am sure some of the Frenchmen thought I looked a bit strange because they kept eyeing me suspiciously.

The journey was uneventful, except when members of the Gestapo entered the carriage to check our documents. Luckily no one spoke a word to them and the Germans noticed nothing unusual, but my heart missed a beat every

"Bon Apres Midi, Gorgeous!"

time I had to produce my forged documents.

At Dax my guide winked at me through the window and walked on slowly to the exit. Several Frenchmen blocked my way as they unloaded their belongings from the luggage rack, and it was several minutes before I could get out of the carriage. When I found my way to the exit my guide was nowhere to be seen. My heart sank to think that having come this far, and so near the Spanish border, I had suddenly lost contact with the people I knew could lead me safely to freedom. However, I was sure my guide would soon reappear to indicate what I should do next, so I sat down on a bench on the deserted platform waiting for something to happen.

After what seemed like an eternity there was still no sign of the guide and the station remained deserted, so there was no point in pretending any longer that I was waiting for another train. I stood up and strolled nervously past the exit gates, which were open with no railway staff in sight. I decided to take the plunge and walked with as much confidence as I could muster through the exit and out towards the centre of town. As no one was there to collect my ticket I still possess it as a momento of this somewhat alarming experience at Dax.

Halfway down the street I saw my guide beckoning frantically from a doorway for me to follow him, putting up a hand to make sure I kept my distance. He led me to a bicycle repair shop and there, inside, were two Americans and one Canadian, who I could swear were the people I had spotted on the platform in Paris. We were to travel together for the rest of the journey through France and over the Pyrenees.

From Dax we travelled south on bicycles which the repair shop provided, first to Bayonne and then to Hendaye. Somewhere along the route we spent a night in a café run by two intrepid ladies who appeared to be English.

I think it was at Bayonne where our guide and the four of us had to cross a bridge guarded by German soldiers. We rode across well spaced out, but once again the Germans noticed nothing suspicious about us or our documents. That evening we were taken to the edge of a wood where our guide

handed us over to a tough Basque smuggler who was to take us over the Pyrenees that night. I thanked our guide profusely and asked him his name so that I could contact him again after the war. He said his name was Franco and with a wink he disappeared into the shadows.

After the war the RAF Escaping Society told me he must have been the Belgian Army Officer, Baron Nothomb, who was one of the heroes of the famous Comet Line escape organisation. I also learnt that the tough Basque smuggler must have been the notorious Florentino who was decorated for taking numerous Allied servicemen over the Pyrenees into Spain.

Florentino led us to a Basque farmhouse near the foothills of the mountains where we washed and fed. Apparently he smuggled radios and valves from Holland across into Spain and brought back silk, soap and American cigarettes on the return journey. We watched him and a colleague packing contraband into rucksacks and they told us we would have to carry some of the lighter ones on our backs as our contribution.

With a mixture of French and sign language they explained we would be taken over a difficult part of the mountains further inland to avoid German and Spanish patrols. We were to walk in single file at three or four yard intervals. We were not to talk or smoke and we were to do whatever we were told. In an emergency it was every man for himself and we couldn't expect help from them because they would be shot if captured.

We were each given a staff and some black bread for the journey before setting off in the pitch darkness for the mountains. The going was tough at times and it was so dark we could only just see the person in front. Each time we reached the top of a ridge there always seemed to be a higher one ahead of us. On one of these we passed a bubbling spring and Florentino allowed us to stop for a drink from a small pool at the side of the path.

At the top of another ridge we could see a dark shape against the skyline. Florentino put up his hand to stop us in our tracks, and we crouched down breathless with our hearts in our mouths. After several minutes Florentino

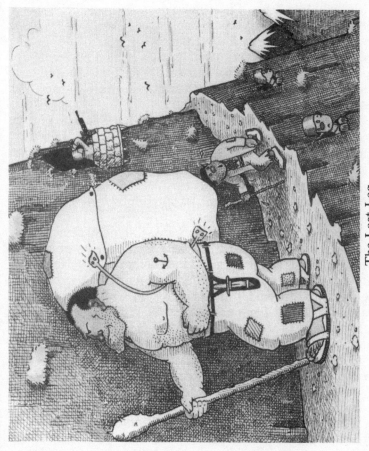

The Last Leg

picked up a stone and threw it at the ghostly figure which, to our relief, turned out to be a mountain pony which galloped past us.

Finally we reached the top of the mountain range to see the most welcome sight of my life. Silhouetted against some further hills were the villages and towns of Spain sprinkled with twinkling lights. Far below us was a stream being swept by searchlights which, presumably, was the River Bridassoa and the French border. Odd flashes of light could also be seen on the other side of the river from the torches of Spanish patrols. Before we started our descent I looked back towards France and the utter darkness. Nazi Europe was blacked out.

We scrambled down the steep slope and crouched in the undergrowth near the bank of the river where we waited while searchlights swept the area several times. Florentino was obviously waiting for the right moment, and at last, immediately one searchlight was doused, he beckoned us to follow him quickly across the icy water which was shallow and narrow at the spot he had chosen.

We scrambled up the further bank and hid in some bushes until Florentino decided it was safe to continue our journey into Spain. We could often see the torches of Spanish patrols but they were far away to the west. As dawn was breaking we were enveloped in mist and fog, so we all sat down to eat some bread and smoke our first cigarette of the journey.

It took a further three hours of hard going before we reached a desolate farmhouse about ten miles inside the border. This was obviously the smugglers' rendevous because we were greeted by some buxom Basque girls, with pitch black hair and pale faces, who gave us wine and rich oily food and looked after the smugglers' comforts.

There were enough beds scattered about for all of us and after too much wine and plenty of food the four of us fell fast asleep while Florentino and his colleague continued their revels. The trek over the Pyrenees had not involved any mountain climbing as such but it was an exhausting experience for anyone doing this sort of thing for the very first time, particularly when carrying a rucksack full of contraband in the pitch dark.

Copy of picture in *The Sphere*. The Padre in the left corner was a Boxing Blue at Oxford but some of us resented this picture because it suggested we always did this before flying which we did not. I was reprimanded by the Station CO for saying so openly!

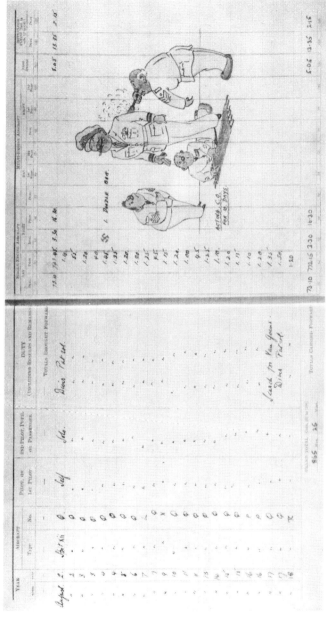

Extract from Pilot's Log Book.

LUCKENWALDE PRISON CAMP

Lunch arriving.

Lunch is taken.

Wooden bunks in the huge Prisoner Blocks at Luckenwalde.

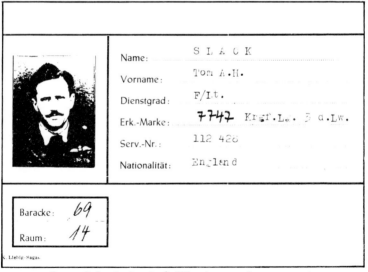

Name:	S L A C K
Vorname:	Tom A.H.
Dienstgrad:	F/Lt.
Erk.-Marke:	7742 Kr.gf.L₃. 3 d.Lw.
Serv.-Nr.:	112 428
Nationalität:	England

Baracke: 69
Raum: 14

K. Liebig-Sagau

Part of the Stalag Luft III prisoner of war records.

1	2	3	4	5	6	7	8	9	10	11	12	13	14	15	16	17	18	19	20	21	22	23	24	25

Personalkarte I: Personelle Angaben

Kriegsgefang. Lager Nr. 3 d. Lw. (Oflag Luft 3)

Beschriftung der Erkennungsmarke
Nr. 7747
Lager Krgsgeflg.d.Lw. 3

Des Kriegsgefangenen

Name: SLACK
Vorname: Tom A. H.
Geburtstag und -ort: Vwgt.
Religion: C of E.
Vorname des Vaters:
Familienname der Mutter:

Staatsangehörigkeit: ENGLAND
Dienstgrad: F/Lt.
Truppenteil: RAF Kom. usw.:
Zivilberuf: Berufs-Gr.:
Matrikel Nr. (Stammrolle des Heimatstaates): 112428
Gefangennahme (Ort und Datum): Hesdin, Frankr. 23.8.44
Ob gesund, krank, verwundet eingeliefert:

Lichtbild

Nähere Personalbeschreibung

Grösse	Haarfarbe
1.78	braun

Besondere Kennzeichen:

Fingerabdruck des rechten ! Zeigefingers

Name und Anschrift der zu benachrichtigenden Person in der Heimat des Kriegsgefangenen 148

T. A. Slack
Uxfeldover
Kent. Eng.

7747 SLACK, T.A.

Beschriftung der Erkennungsmarke Nr. Lager: Name:

Bemerkungen:

Personalbeschreibung

Figur:
Größe: 1.78
Alter:
Gesichtsform:
Gesichtsfarbe:
Schädelform:
Augen:
Nase:
Gebiß:
Haare:
Bart:
Gewicht: kg
Besondere Merkmale:
Deutsche Sprachkenntnisse:

Prisoner of war record card from Stalag Luft III.

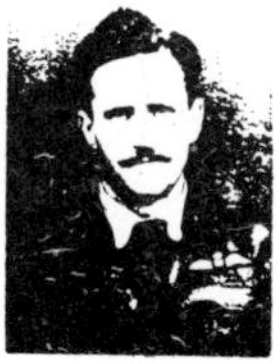

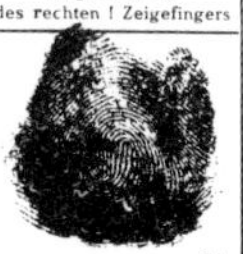

41 Squadron Spitfire – probably flown by F/Lt Don Smith.

Self in Borneo in peace time. The best picture of
me ever taken — at the time I did not know, but I
was simply covered in jungle leeches.

The Prisoner of War

WE SALUTE YOU AND WISH YOU THE VERY BEST OF LUCK ! One repatriate who received this message from the British and Dominions Red Crosses in his gift bag drew this picture on the back of the card and posted it to the Red Cross in London.

NO! WE· SALUTE AND THANK YOU !

Thanks Again !

Just a few of the many letters we have received

Thanks offered by the author to the Red Cross.

After the war I was to tackle a mountain in real earnest when Pat Sheehy, Freddie Almond and I decided to climb Mount Cameroon before launching a new brand of cigarettes in the area in 1953. Mount Cameroon is over 13,000 feet high which meant spending a night near the top before climbing to the summit the next morning. The District Officer at Buea provided a guide to lead us to a derelict hut on the side of the mountain where we could shelter for the night, and he told us to report to him the moment we returned otherwise he would have to organise a search party because the mountain was often enveloped in cloud and it was easy to get lost.

When we reached the summit early on the second day, Freddie Almond produced a bottle of champagne which he had somehow managed to hide inside his outer clothing. When he opened it the altitude caused the cork to go flying up another hundred feet or so, followed by a snaking column of froth. There was barely any champagne left to drink but we used the bottle to leave a note inside, recording our names and the date, and placed it in a cache of stones on the top of the mountain.

Late that night, when we finally reached the foot of the mountain, we staggered into the District Officer's house to report our safe return, soaking wet, utterly exhausted, with blisters and bleeding feet. We were bursting to tell him all about our moment of triumph, until he greeted us excitedly with the BBC news that Hillary and Tenzing had just climbed Everest.

After resting and spending the night at the Basque farmhouse, Florentino led us early the next day to a village several miles away which was on the main road to San Sebastian on the West Coast of Spain.

On the way to the village we still had to be careful of the Spanish patrols because Franco's government was pro-German and Fascist, but luckily the anti-Franco Basques were not.

We encountered several of these patrols, consisting of two members of the Civil Guard in their funny patent leather hats, but we could hear them miles away as they talked excitedly to each other, which allowed us to hide behind bushes until they had passed.

Once in the Basque village we felt relatively free at last, although our French documents would probably have been of little use if we had been stopped and questioned in Spain.

We were then taken on public transport to San Sebastian where we were hidden in a flat owned by two Basque ladies, until we could be whisked away by staff from our respective Embassies. I was driven quite openly to Madrid to be hidden in a building in the British Embassy grounds, which appeared to be a Sanctuary for all sorts of fugitives. I was then driven to Seville for the final leg of the journey to Gibraltar and freedom.

I was given a sherry or two and something to eat at a café near the harbour. My companion from the Embassy told me I would have to slide down a coal chute into the hold of a Norwegian ship which we could see from the café. He would take me up a ladder to the cabin at the top of the chute and at a given signal the operator would stop the conveyor belt supplying the coal. I was then to plummet down the chute feet first to the coal heap in the hold where a Norwegian sailor would be waiting in the shadows. The moment I landed I was to scramble over to him quickly because the supply of coal could only be stopped for a few seconds without causing suspicion.

Everything went according to plan and sure enough there was the Norwegian waiting at the side of the hold. I scrambled towards him and within seconds coal was pouring out of the chute once more. He led me sweating and covered in coal dust, to a hiding-place in the bowels of the ship at the stern in the propeller shaft tunnel, where I had to squat in the dark on duck-boards which were being lapped by bilge water.

The Norwegian told me he was sorry, but I would have to remain there until the Spanish officials left the ship after it reached the mouth of the estuary and the open sea, about 25 miles or so down river. He said I was not to worry because he would soon be bringing me some food and water, but Ships' Regulations compelled him to close the watertight doors so it might get a little stuffy.

When my eyes got accustomed to the darkness I noticed I was not alone. There was someone else in the tunnel, but try as I might I couldn't find out who or what he was, although he was very pleasant and polite. When the ship reached the open sea he was led away first in the dark before they came back for me, and I didn't catch a glimpse of him during the voyage.

When I finally reached the deck I was filthy, and the heat and coal dust had made me come out in a rash from head to foot. After breathing the refreshing sea air for a moment or two, I was taken below for a steaming hot bath and a change of clothing. They even washed and ironed the spotted red scarf which I had worn throughout my travels. It had been given to me by my younger sister, Midge, in the WRNS, to bring me luck. She had been stationed in Gibraltar when I left England, and there was every chance she would still be there when I arrived.

When we anchored off Gibraltar a smallish man wearing civilian clothes and dark glasses was taken hurriedly down the gangplank into an impressive Naval launch with a Senior Officer on board. As the launch pulled away he looked up and gave me a little wave. He must have been the person in the shaft tunnel, and one could only guess that he was some sort of spy.

Eventually they took me ashore where the local British Intelligence began checking my identity. I had several recorded scars and chopped off toes to prove who I was, but to save time I told them about my sister in the WRNS who could easily vouch for me if she was still on the Rock. They checked to confirm that she was, so I was escorted to the building where she worked. I asked a Wren to take the red scarf into her office and say that the owner was waiting to see her outside.

She came rushing out and flung her arms around me. British Intelligence was satisfied and I spent a wonderful three days with my sister and her Wren friends, until I was flown back to England in a blacked-out vintage Dakota.

Before going home to Micheldever and on to London for some leave, I went down to Tangmere for a night to celebrate with the Squadron. They told me that our Wing Commander had shot down the two Messerschmitts he had chased on that day in July, but the Squadron had lost Dickie Hogarth who had been shot down and killed.

Before leaving, I went to see the WAAF who had packed my parachute to give her the customary kiss and a one pound note, which was a lot of money in those days, and I sent off an application to join the Caterpillar Club run by the makers of our parachutes for anyone who had saved their life by baling out.

My elder sister, Rosemary, in the VAD, gave me a beautiful pewter tankard inscribed with the date July 18th, 1943 to remind me to be more careful in future each time I raised the tankard to my lips, which she knew would be fairly frequent.

9

LECTURE TOUR, D-DAY AND A DIP IN THE SEA

It had taken me thirty days to reach Gibraltar, which was
considered pretty good going until a Polish pilot, who was
an expert linguist, made the journey in about ten days,
after boarding the first train south without any help or
documents or anything.

However, RAF Intelligence still thought it was worth-
while sending me on a lecture tour of all fighter stations,
after giving me a test at their secret Head Quarters somewhere in the suburbs of London. This tour lasted six weeks
and took me all over England, Wales, Northern Ireland and
Scotland, and even included some lonely RAF outposts
in the outer Scottish Islands.

Once I had to talk to a Free French Squadron who were
not interested in how to escape because most of them had
done so already. All they wanted to know was about
conditions in occupied France, and how the Germans were
treating their people. I told them what I could and tried to
reassure them. As far as other squadrons were concerned,
I tended to concentrate on the more humorous side of
escaping, and I hope no one baled out as a result, expecting
a continental holiday. Humour was very much a part of
Squadron life, even under conditions of extreme stress,
and there were endless humorous stories about the RAF —
some of them true and some of them possibly not.

There was the story about the crew of a Wellington
Bomber which had been badly hit by flak on a raid over
Germany. The instrument panel had been shattered but

77

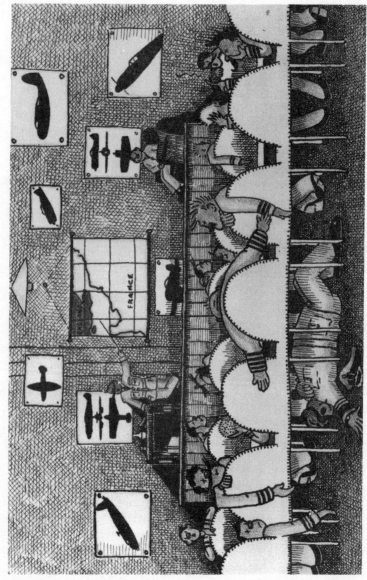

Lecturing to RAF Stations on Escaping

the pilot managed to keep the aircraft flying in what his navigator thought was the direction of home. One engine was losing power and after a time the aircraft started to lose height. It broke cloud over some desolate open country at only a thousand feet, so the pilot decided he would have to make an emergency landing. He chose the largest field he could find and crash-landed. The pilot and crew were unhurt and, after setting fire to the aircraft, they ran into a wood to hide from the enemy.

After a few days they ran out of the emergency rations they had salvaged from the aircraft, so they decided to emerge from the wood to seek help. They saw a man working in a field so they approached him cautiously. He looked at them suspiciously while the pilot tried to explain in broken French that they were RAF, their plane had crashed, and they wanted to get back to England. He listened carefully but couldn't understand a word. Finally he pushed back his cap, scratched his head and exclaimed, "Cor blimey, a bunch of bloody foreigners." They had landed in Kent.

There was another story about two famous high-ranking twins in the regular RAF who were flying in separate aircraft one day when they spotted a yellow training aircraft in front of them. They were in radio contact with each other and decided to play one of their tricks on the poor pupil pilot. They turned their aircraft over and flew on either side of him upside down. The pupil pilot looked from one to the other and decided in panic that he must be the wrong way up, so he turned his aircraft over and promptly went into a spin, only managing to pull out at tree top level.

There is also the ridiculous story about the Air Marshal who went to inspect an RAF Coastal Command Station where he was taken up for a flight in one of the Squadron's Flying Boats. When the plane was airborne the pilot let him take over the controls and suggested he might also like to do a practice landing. The Air Marshal was delighted and immediately turned inland and started his approach towards the runway of a fighter station. When the pilot hurriedly pointed out that they were in a Flying Boat, the Air Marshal pulled back the stick and headed towards the coast where he landed safely in the estuary alongside the Coastal Command Station. As he walked to the door of the plane he turned to the pilot and said, somewhat tersely, that of course he knew it was a Flying Boat and he had merely been testing the pilot's reactions. With that, he stepped out of the door and fell slap into the sea.

Then there was the old chestnut about the Polish pilot who couldn't get a reply on the RT from his English No. 2 flying alongside him. Finally in desperation he shouted into his mouthpiece, "Eef you are not receiving me for Christ's sake vaggle your vings."

There was a wonderful American in our Squadron called Waggie, short for Herbert J. Wagner, Junior, and when his country came into the war he was offered the rank of Colonel in the US Air Force, at about ten times his RAF salary, but nothing could tempt him away from the Squadron. He had a great sense of humour but could never see anything funny in *Punch*. One day he saw me laughing while reading the latest issue so he came over to see what was causing so much amusement. I showed him a drawing by George Morrow of two Roman soldiers building Hadrian's Wall. One was carrying a huge boulder on his shoulders and he was turning to his companion and asking "Why can't someone invent a wheelbarrow?" Waggie gave me the coldest of looks and obviously thought I was some sort of nutcase.

During the lecture tour I gave a talk at a station in Cornwall where I met Mary Crear, the most beautiful WAAF Officer I had ever seen. At long last I felt I had met the girl of my dreams, and we spent all our leaves together until I was forced down to become a prisoner of war. She was also responsible for saving my life when I parachuted into the sea off the French coast, but more about this later.

I ended the lecture tour in Northern Ireland and on one occasion, when travelling by train to Londonderry, the locomotive ran out of steam and broke down. There was an indomitable old lady in the carriage who started to organise everything and everybody, including the train driver and guard who kept saluting her. She turned out to be the mother of the famous General Montgomery, who had obviously inherited some of her formidable character.

On my return to the Squadron I was promoted to Flight

Lieutenant and given command of a Flight, under a marvellous CO called Pinkie Glen. These were to be some of my happiest days in the Squadron.

During this time I was sent to test the new 'Tear Drop' hood for Spitfires at High Post aerodrome where I met the plane's famous test pilot, Jeffrey Quill, for the first time. This hood enabled pilots to look behind to watch their tails and a very successful test was only marred by the fact that I nearly crashed the Naval Spitfire XV involved because Jeffrey had failed to tell me that the air speed indicator was expressed in knots compared with my accustomed miles per hour.

In April 1944 the Squadron was posted to Bolt Head in 10 Group. This airfield was on the hill behind Hope Cove in Devon where we were billeted in the large hotel overlooking the small bay with its fishing boats, lobster pots and local pub. There was a great deal of military and naval activity in the West Country at this time, and it was our job to intercept the German reconnaissance planes which were taking too keen an interest in the area.

Once we had started our patrols the reconnaissance aircraft kept away so we were sent on sweeps and rhubarbs over the Brest Peninsular. These involved too long a flight over water for comfort in a single-engined aircraft and we lost five Spitfires in the sea during our short stay at Bolt Head. Robbie was killed, Waggie was picked up by Germans off Jersey and taken prisoner, but three of us were lucky enough to rejoin the Squadron thanks to the Air Sea Rescue Service.

The military and naval build-up in the area increased, and from the air we could see tanks, guns, troops and transport everywhere, with ships, boats and landing craft filling the creeks and estuaries. No wonder the German reconnaissance planes had taken such an interest. There was no hiding the fact, the long awaited D-Day and invasion of Europe could not be far away. Then, on June 6th, the invasion started, and D-Day had arrived at last.

The Squadron took off at dawn to provide fighter cover over the beachhead, but luckily we were only required to make one flight over the area that first day because the whole world seemed to be there and, like Dieppe, confusion reigned.

In the general mêlée no one appeared to know who was friend or foe, and the Americans were the worst culprits who fired at everything and anything in sight, shooting down Jack Refshauge into the sea and giving him the Purple Heart as their idea of compensation.

After the war a magnificent tapestry was commissioned by Lord Dulverton to depict the D-Day landings in Normandy. The Royal School of Needlework undertook the work which took three years to complete, using a lot of young talent who had not even been born at the time and didn't know what a tin hat or gas mask looked like. The tapestry used to be housed proudly in the Whitbread brewery offices in Chiswell Street, London EC1, and when I went there one day long after the war to admire it, I found that all the Spitfires shown flying over the invading armada carried our Squadron's markings.

I immediately telephoned the Royal School of Needlework to find out why our Squadron had been so honoured. They put me in touch with a Miss Bartlett who said the school had been advised by what they called the three wise men from the Navy, the Army and the Air Force. Unfortunately the wise man from the Air Force was now dead, but I believe the Spitfire models for the tapestry may have come from a very popular jigsaw puzzle after the war which showed a colour picture of several of our Squadron's aircraft flying in immaculate formation. Those of us who had seen the original photograph knew that some aircraft had been moved fractionally forward and others fractionally backwards, and one which had been badly out of formation had been erased completely, to give possibly the best picture of perfect formation flying of all time.

The tapestry is now housed in the D-Day museum at Southsea, but experts will have noticed that the Spitfires lack the black and white stripes carried by Allied aircraft during the landings which supports the theory that the Spitfires were copied from the jigsaw puzzle which appeared long before D-Day.

Life had become pretty hectic for the Squadron, operating daily over this dangerous corner of France, but I was due for twenty-four hours leave, so I flew our Tiger Moth to Portreath in Cornwall to spend my leave with Mary.

A few days after returning from leave, there had been a particularly lively celebration down at the local pub, and one of the pilots in my flight who was due to fly on a shipping reconnaissance at dawn the next day returned very much the worse for wear. I told him to go to bed to sleep it off and I would take his place the next morning.

I had had a few beers myself so I retired to bed early. It was hot and humid and I spent a restless night having vivid dreams. I was called well before dawn with a cup of hot tea by a grand old batman called Jock who looked after us like a father. As I sat up rubbing my eyes I asked him what happened to pilots who crashed in the sea. He was a God fearing man and said they would meet the Lord their Maker. I told him this wasn't necessarily so because I had just had a dream about being in the sea, and the next thing I knew I was back in the local pub drinking beer with all my friends in the Squadron.

It was June the 18th, and a day to remember. The shipping reconnaissance that day was to be from St. Malo to the Island of Ouessant, or Ushant, and my No. 2 was to be a Sergeant in the Royal Australian Air Force called Ware who had just joined the Squadron.

We met plenty of flak along the French coast and I heard some of it hitting my aircraft. I noticed the fuel gauge was dropping quickly to zero and within a few minutes the engine spluttered and stopped. I just had time to give a few quick 'maydays' over the radio before turning the aircraft onto its back to bale out.

This time there was no problem as I shot out of the cockpit, pulled the rip cord and floated down towards the sea near the Island of Ushant. I remembered to hit the parachute's safety release the moment my feet touched the water, so that I would surface away from the parachute without becoming entangled in the silk and the cords.

As I came up for air, the small fighter dinghy attached to the parachute harness had inflated automatically and I clambered aboard, sitting there shivering while waiting to be rescued. The sea around the dinghy had become bright yellow from the pouch of chemicals which was attached to

In the Drink

my Mae West. This was to assist searching aircraft because a small dinghy, particularly in rough seas, would be difficult to see.

Suddenly I saw some stained pound notes floating by which must have fallen out of my pockets as I hit the water. I paddled furiously with my hands to retrieve them, but the ripples from the moving dinghy kept pushing them further out of reach. Anyway, there were more serious problems on my mind, so I sat back in the dinghy searching the sky in the hope of seeing a British aircraft.

It must have been about this time that Mary Crear came on duty in the Operation's Room at Portreath. I learnt later that when she arrived she asked if there was anything exciting to report and was told that there was a 'Whaler Blue One' in the sea off Ushant. She knew 'Whaler' was the 41 Squadron call sign and Blue was my flight, so she asked who the pilot was. No one knew but it was easy to check, so the WAAF telephoned the dispersal hut at Bolt Head to find out.

When Mary was told who it was, she used all her charm, beauty and influence to launch a veritable armada of aircraft and rescue launches into the area. My dinghy was first spotted by an Air Sea Rescue Warwick aircraft which radioed my position back to Portreath and dropped smoke floats to mark the spot clearly. Before long the air was humming with aircraft dropping more smoke floats until it was difficult to breathe, and then a Sunderland dropped a large dinghy within a few feet of my own. I climbed aboard but tied my small dinghy alongside in case of emergency.

An Air Sea Rescue Walrus arrived and landed in the sea to take me on board, and who should I see waving from the back but Sergeant Ware, who had baled out in the middle of the Channel. Apparently he had seen my aircraft hit the water but had not seen my parachute, so he had climbed to a suitable height to send 'maydays' to Portreath. It was his 'maydays' which had been received because mine were sent too low over the sea. He had then circled around looking for me and had run out of fuel before he could get back to base.

The sea was not rough but there was a large swell and the Walrus couldn't get airborne. Luckily, an RAF Air Sea Rescue launch appeared and took the two of us on board. The

Walrus jettisoned all unnecessary equipment and, with the launch zigzagging at speed in front of it to help calm the swell, the plane finally managed to take off.

The launch then returned to the scene to fire its machine guns to sink the dinghies, and the crew retrieved my parachute which would make lovely silk underwear for their wives and sweethearts on shore.

The crew gave us warm clothes and huge tots of rum, and within a few minutes we were fast asleep on bunks in the cabin. We were put ashore safely in Newlyn harbour, just below where I now live, where Mary had RAF transport waiting to take us to Portreath. Before climbing the hill to the aerodrome we stopped outside the WAAF officers' quarters to see if Mary was off duty. She was waiting and we had a very emotional reunion indeed.

Sergeant Ware and I returned to Hope Cove to celebrate in the local pub that evening. Apparently no one was particularly worried about us because Jock had told everyone about the conversation that morning, and he had promised we would be back in the pub before nightfall.

I was told, somewhat belatedly, that there was a poem about Ushant which ran as follows:

'Qui voit Ouessant,
voit son sang.
Qui voit Groix
voit son Croix.'

I must remember to avoid Groix, wherever it is. If nothing else, the baling out and the dip in the sea made me a double member of the Caterpillar Club, and also a member of the Goldfish Club run by the makers of our inflatable dinghies.

10

PRISONER OF WAR

Within a few days our Squadron was transferred back to 11 Group to operate from Friston, a grass airfield on top of Beachy Head. We had been there for a short time previously, to discourage tip and run raids, but this time our role was to be very different.

We had known for some time that the Germans were developing some sort of secret weapon, because we had often escorted bombers to drop their loads on what looked like camouflaged launching sites along the Northern coast of France. The Allies were slowly advancing through France and the Russians were on the offensive, so Hitler decided to launch his secret weapons on the civilian population of London and Southern England in a last desperate effort to avoid defeat.

None of us knew what these weapons were until V1s, or flying bombs, started clattering over the South coast on their way to London. Their fuel was designed to run out as the bomb approached its target and, when the engine stopped, the clattering changed to deadly silence as the bomb went into a dive to explode indiscriminately on populated areas.

Next came the V2 rockets which could only be heard coming after they had arrived with a deafening explosion.

With our clipped-wing Spitfires and powerful Griffon engines, the Squadron stood a good chance of shooting down these doodlebugs, or buzz bombs as the V1s were soon to be called. However, they were usually pretty fast, and we could only catch them if we spotted them from

Doodlebugs

above and could dive down at speed to fire from dead astern. Sometimes they would blow up in front of the aircraft when hit with cannon, and it was then safest for the pilot to fly through the blast, and not turn away exposing the belly of the aircraft to all the flying metal. At other times they would dive out of control with the engine still clattering away, which must have been a frightening experience for people on the ground. The stories about pilots flying alongside the slower or damaged ones and tipping them over with their wings were true, but I think Terry Spencer was the only person in our Squadron to do this, although Joe Birbeck would have done so if given half the chance.

Terry was married in London whilst at Friston with us. His bride was the famous and beautiful actress Lesley Brooke whose brother, Babe Learoyd, won the VC on a daring bomber raid early in the war.

I returned from one scramble to report to Gizzy that I thought I had shot down a doodlebug in the Ashford area but I had not seen it hit the ground. He made a few phone calls and was told a doodlebug had exploded half an hour ago in the middle of the Ashford Railway Yards, causing considerable damage to railway property and military equipment destined for the Front in Europe. We both hurriedly agreed not to claim it as shot down by me or anyone else in 41 Squadron.

After this unfortunate incident Gizzy said that if Hitler ever heard about all the British equipment I had been responsible for destroying, like the Audax in the desert, the Spitfires in France and in the Channel, and now the marshalling yards at Ashford, he would probably award me the Iron Cross First Class with diamonds and crossed swords. Little did he know that there was soon to be another Spitfire to add to this shameful list.

From Friston we were transferred to Lympe, near Hythe, because the doodlebugs were now coming further east along the coast. At Friston we had been billeted in a lovely old house in a valley called Friston Place with a large well in the garden. We used to throw coins in the well to bring us luck, so whoever lives there now could be sitting on a hoard of wartime silver and copper. At Lympe we lived in equal luxury in an exotic mansion belonging to the Sassoon family, which had sunken baths with gold taps, and all sorts of intriguing connecting doors between the bedrooms.

One of my great friends in the Squadron was Prince Emanuel Galitzine. He started the war fighting with the Finns against the Soviets, before joining the RAF where he sometimes flew on operations when not acting as a glamorous ADC to one Air Marshal or another. His father was so grateful for the help given by the British to his family at the time of the Russian Revolution, that he told his three sons at the outbreak of the war that the eldest must join the Navy, the middle one the Army, and Emanuel, the youngest, the RAF.

Before joining the Squadron, Emanuel and his Army brother, George, thought up the idea of making the Germans think the Russian Air Force was operating from England. Emanuel would fly a Spitfire along the French coast talking Russian to George who replied from an Ops room in Fighter Command. The first few flights were uneventful, but subsequent ones caused just about the whole of the German Luftwaffe to get airborne and head for Emanuel's Spitfire. For his own safety the experiment had to be hurriedly abandoned, so Emanuel is alive to this day and remains a very close friend and Godfather to my beautiful daughter.

Chasing doodlebugs entailed continuous patrols and long hours of readiness, so Fighter Command decided to send us on a sweep to make a welcome change. It was August the 23rd and I was due for twenty-four hours leave and had arranged to fly to Portreath in the Squadron Tiger Moth to see Mary. However, the weather in Cornwall was bad, so Flying Control told me to postpone the trip until conditions in the West Country improved. I therefore decided to lead my Flight on this sweep because it was over the Amiens area which I knew so well from the air and also on the ground. Fighter pilots were superstitious about flying on a day off, and everyone reminded me of this on the way to the dispersal hut.

We took off with a new CO called Chapman, with Terry Spencer leading his Flight and with me leading mine. No one expected much activity because the Luftwaffe were too busy coping with advancing armies elsewhere, so we carried drop tanks to give extra range in case the Ops Room decided to divert us to another area.

When the fuel in our drop tanks was nearly exhausted, the CO gave the sign for all of us to jettison them simultaneously to increase our speed and improve manoeuvrability. Mine went sailing down with the others, but the Bowden cable failed to switch the fuel supply over to the main tank, and the engine soon spluttered and stopped.

I was losing height, with everyone telling me what to do over the RT, which I jolly well knew like the back of my hand, but none of the emergency drill seemed to work. As far as we knew, Rex, Haybag and Leslie had gone missing in our Squadron for the same reason, due to a fault in the cable or an airlock somewhere.

By this time the aircraft was too low for me to bale out, so I crash-landed in a field near Hesdin, knocking myself out. When I came to, a few seconds later, there were two German soldiers with rifles standing on the wing of the Spitfire. One of them was screaming for me to get "Aus, Aus," so I asked him politely to jolly well help me 'Aus'.

I had crashed alongside a camouflaged searchlight battery. There was no Mary or French Underground to help me now and I was put in a deep slit trench, with two armed guards looking down on me. They appeared fed up with the war, and kept stressing that they were Austrians and not Germans. They asked if my red scarf meant I was a Communist. They knew the Allies had just taken Paris, only a hundred and fifty miles or so away, and said they hoped that the war would soon be over. I told them I would put in a good word for them if they turned their backs and let me make a run for it, but they didn't think this at all funny.

Now and again an NCO would come over to look at me and then their behaviour would change completely, with lots of heel clicking and "Heil Hitler's". When left in peace, I watched the Allied bombers and fighters which seemed to be continually overhead. Lucky people, they would soon be home for tea. Mary would soon be having hers. I kept thinking of her, not knowing that I was never to see her again.

91

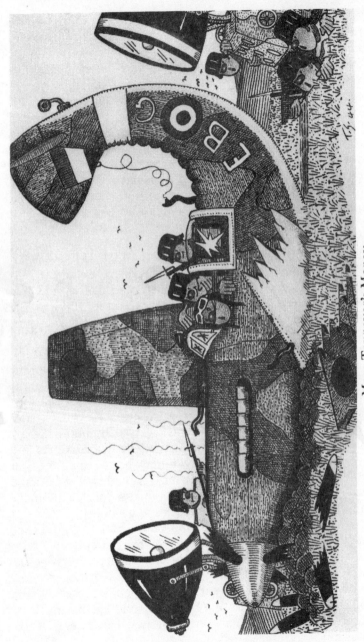

More Taxpayer's Money

Before long two Germans arrived on a motor-cycle and sidecar. They bundled me into the sidecar while the second German rode pillion, and drove me off to Battery Headquarters. Here I was guarded closely until two members of the Luftwaffe arrived who searched me and removed all my possessions, which luckily were next to nothing.

They took me in a Volkswagen to a nearby aerodrome, with me in the front sitting next to the driver, and with his colleague squashed in the back, holding a tommy-gun between the two front seats. Suddenly we hit a bump and the tommy-gun went off, spraying the dashboard with bullets and covering the driver with debris. He jammed on the brakes, and both of them started shouting and cursing at me, but this was nothing compared to the fright I had when the bullets went whistling past my shoulder.

At the aerodrome I spent the night in a cell and early next morning I was driven to a civilian gaol in Lille, where I was treated worse than a common criminal. The cells were filthy, with plain boards to sleep on, and a pail in the corner as the only permitted latrine.

The next day I was escorted to the Station and put on a train for Brussels. Two badly injured American airmen were on the train. One had suffered terrible burns and his legs and arms were wrapped in paper bandages covered in ointment, with some bare bones plainly visible. Their guards had taken compassion on them and they were stretched out on the soft seats of a second class compartment.

Suddenly two German officers appeared, shouting something about murderers and terror bombers, and they had the three of us and our guards moved the length of the train to the van at the back, where the poor Americans had to lie on the floor. Some German women in uniform on the train literally winced as the Americans hobbled painfully down the corridor, helped by their shamefaced guards.

On arrival in Brussels, the Americans were taken to a hospital and I spent the day in a huge gaol overlooking the river, where at least I was given some bread and soup, which was a welcome relief because people kept forgetting to feed me. That night I was escorted back to the station again to take a train to the Luftwaffe's Interrogation Centre at Dulag

Alone with One's Thoughts

94

Luft, near Frankfurt in Germany.

On arrival there all prisoners were stripped naked and given a hot shower while their clothes were fumigated. When my clothes were returned my red scarf was missing so I refused to dress. There was a lot of heated argument, but the guards refused to fetch the scarf, so I still refused to budge. I was sitting naked on a wooden bench when an officer arrived to explain that the scarf was not part of my uniform and, according to the Geneva Convention, the Germans were right to confiscate it. I tried to explain that it was given to me by my sister to bring me luck, and I had worn it throughout the war. Finally in desperation the officer told the guard to retrieve it and, honour satisfied, I started to put on my uniform.

This was a typical example of the inexplicable behaviour of Germans. If this had been a British Camp with German prisoners, the prisoner would have been told to get dressed or receive a bayonet up the backside. The British are basically humane but stand no nonsense, whereas the Germans can be ruthless and cruel but want to be thought human.

I had always been in trouble at school for my obstinacy, and when my father had received a particularly bad report in far away Siam about me from my Prep School, the Elms in Colwall, he asked Oliver Baldwin to go down to sort things out. Oliver was the Socialist son and heir of the Conservative Prime Minister, Stanley Baldwin, and he had been a sort of guardian during my holidays when my parents were away in the Far East. He visited the Elms and got on famously with the Headmaster, W.P. Singleton, and sent the following poem to my father and mother, Violet, without a covering letter or further comment:

SCHOOL REPORT
I went to the 'Elms'
To see young Tom.
He is happy and well
And has done no wrong.

Singleton's nice.
He's fond of the lad.

95

He wouldn't be that
If the boy had been bad.

Please worry no more
About that and this.
Your son is all right.
Give Violet a kiss.

I was amazed to be told later that my guardian was a homosexual because he never gave me any cause to think or even suspect this, although once, at his house in Princes Risborough, I remember his father and mother giving me some very strange sideways glances. On another occasion, I remember him arranging for me to spend a few nights away, which I now presume was for my protection, while he held a weekend party for a group of well known authors, playwrights, fashion designers and society columnists who were obviously of a similar bent.

The guard, who obviously was never going to forgive me about the red scarf, led me to a cell where I was to spend the next seven days while the Germans tried to soften me up for interrogation. What follows formed part of a BBC Radio 4 programme called 'Prisoners of War' compiled by David Wade.

The cell was small and austere, consisting of a radiator, a small table, a wooden bed with straw mattress and a blanket, and a high window with bars. It was still summer and the window was open, the radiator off, and conditions were tolerable.

After a few minutes the guard appeared again and closed the window, ignoring my protests. He pointed at a lever by the door saying that if I wanted anything I should pull the lever and an arm would drop down in the passage to attract his attention. After he had left, he switched on the radiator from somewhere outside, and the cell started to become unbearably hot.

When a prisoner pulled his lever the guard would slowly stomp down the passage in his jackboots and stop outside the door of the cell. After a long pause he would push the arm back into place and stomp slowly back up the passage again. This infuriating situation would continue for about three days, with the prisoner receiving only water and no food.

Then someone in civilian clothes would be ushered into the cell, and the conversation would go something like this:

"Good God, what on earth is going on? This cell is unbearably hot."

"Of course it is. The guard has shut the window, turned the radiator on, and it's the middle of summer. What's more, they are starving me to death."

"Oh, these Germans! Never mind, I'm a Swiss from the Red Cross and I can soon fix this, but first I need a few details, so that I can tell your family and loved ones that you are safe."

He would then start asking all sorts of questions like, "What is your Squadron?", "What aircraft were you flying?", "Where were you stationed?" and so on.

We had been briefed that the Geneva Convention only required a prisoner to give his name, rank and number and nothing more, so I kept repeating, "My name is Slack, my rank is Flight Lieutenant, and my number is 112428." My visitor became more and more impatient, and said he wouldn't be able to help me or send a message to England unless I agreed to be more co-operative. Finally, he became furious and stomped out of the cell. He was obviously no Swiss from any Red Cross.

The next day I was visited by what appeared to be a charming officer from the Luftwaffe. When I complained about the conditions in the cell, he called the guard and ordered him to open the windows, switch off the radiator, and bring me something to eat. He sat on the bed while I polished off a bowl of hot soup, and when I had finished he gave me a cigarette and lit it for me.

He apologised for my treatment, explaining that the guards were soldiers in the Reichswehr and not airmen, so they knew nothing of the chivalry which existed between the Luftwaffe and the RAF. Then the questions started all over again, but he didn't seem too surprised when I kept repeating my name, rank and number. In fact he remained very pleasant throughout the visit and, before

e

leaving, he placed some cigarettes and a box of matches on the table beside my bed.

As soon as he had left, the guard stormed in to shut the window, grab my cigarettes and matches, and slam the door as he left. Any minute I knew the radiator would start radiating. This really was the end and I lay fuming on my bed. The Germans must have decided I was ready for the real thing, so I was led next morning to the main interrogation centre in the compound.

The interrogation officer wore Luftwaffe uniform and also appeared to be a very friendly and pleasant individual, who stood up as I entered the room. Again the conversation went something like this:

"Please sit down and make yourself comfortable. A cigarette?"

"Thank you."

"A light?"

"Thank you."

"How are they treating you over at the house?"

"Over at the what?"

"You know what I mean."

"Disgracefully."

"Have they given you any food?"

"No, except for one plate of something, and you know it."

"I'm sorry. I can soon fix that, but first we must have one or two personal particulars. What Squadron were you in?"

"My name is Slack, my rank is . . ."

"Come on, you've already given us all that, but what was your Squadron?"

"You know my Squadron because I crashed my aircraft, and the Squadron letters are painted on the side."

"I must warn you we believe you to be a spy."

"What nonsense. I was captured in the cockpit of my aircraft, wearing RAF uniform."

"What better way to enter France?"

This was the old, old trick. The word spy was always frightening because the penalty was the firing squad, and it was difficult to prove innocence without giving something away. Luckily he suddenly changed the subject.

"You escaped once, didn't you?"

This took me completely by surprise. "How on earth do you know that?"

"Someone put your name as missing in the personal columns of the Telegraph or the Times or somewhere. It's lucky France has been overrun by your armies, or we would want to know how you got away."

He suddenly ceased to question me, and offered me a lager and another cigarette. He obviously knew that the war would soon be over and he even asked me if I would give him a letter to say that he had treated me decently. I said I couldn't do that, but he was free to mention my name if captured and I would put in a good word. He thanked me and called the guard, who took me back to my cell. The window was open, the radiator was off, and within a few minutes I was brought a proper meal.

The interrogators had had enough and, after only seven days at Dulag Luft, I was told I was to be transferred to Stalag Luft 3 which was the famous camp for RAF officers in Silesia. It was just as well I was not kept longer at Dulag Luft, because this would have meant I was giving away useful information, and questions would have been asked at home after the war was over.

Those of us who were due to leave Dulag Luft were marshalled together in a yard before being sent to our respective POW camps. I was amazed to see how many of us there were, because while in solitary confinement I had imagined that I was the only person in the place. We were formed up into a squad of British, Commonwealth and American Air Force officers, and I was instructed by the Germans to be the leader. A German officer approached and asked for my word of honour not to try to escape or allow any of the group to do so. When I explained that this was impossible because it was an officer's duty to escape, he said that in that case all our belts, braces and laces would have to be removed. This resulted in loud boos and catcalls from the American contingent telling me to 'cut the crap' and asking the Germans to appoint another leader. This they did to my satisfaction and everyone else's, so that we were able to be marched properly attired to the local railway station.

On arrival at Sagan, I was interrogated and vetted by a small group of senior British officers before being allotted to room 14 in hut 69. This was because the room housed the camp's secret radio and transmitter, and no one was taking any chances.

The radio was hidden in bits and pieces all over the room, but it could be assembled in seconds each night to receive the BBC news. When the radio was in use, prisoners would keep guard outside the door and at each end of the hut, and at the slightest warning, it could be taken to pieces and hidden again in seconds. The brain behind this operation was a civilian boffin named Howard Cundall from the Ministry of Defence. He was shot down over France in a Wellington which contained secret equipment to bend the beams used to guide German bombers onto their targets in Britain. Luckily he was wearing a type of blue battledress at the time, and was able to convince his captors that he was only an RAF Officer somewhat improperly dressed.

Some of the prisoners who vetted me had been in prison for years, and they were eager to know when the war would be over. I told them it would definitely be over by Christmas. They said this was nonsense and that they had heard such stories many times before. They appeared so despondent that I promised to run round the camp naked on Christmas Day if I was proved wrong, wearing nothing more than a blue ribbon tied round a certain part of my anatomy. This appeared to cheer them up. At least it showed that I seemed to believe what I said, and I was not to know that temperatures can reach 20° below zero or more in Sagan in December.

POW's in Sagan referred to themselves as Kriegies, which is short for the German mouthful Kriegsgefangenen, and the German guards were known as Goons, or as Ferrets if they were one of those operating inside the camp looking for tunnels, radios, or anything else suspicious. Sagan was where the famous Wooden Horse escape took place, and also the mass escape later when Hitler ordered everyone recaptured to be shot. After this massacre all officers at Sagan were released from their duty to escape, because the war was nearly over and it would have been a waste of human life.

The camp consisted of rows of large wooden huts with a door, a cooking stove and a wash place at one end, and another door at the bottom of a corridor at the other end. Leading off from the corridor were twenty rooms, each containing ten or twelve officers. Prisoners were supplied with one Red Cross food parcel per week to supplement the German rations, and even when this was reduced to half a parcel, when German supply lines became disorganised, it was still enough to keep everyone fit and happy. There was a roster for each room to have the use of the cooking stoves once or twice a week, so that a room's duty cook could prepare a special dish or a huge iced cake, made from the contents of our food parcels. Some prisoners even made brandy secretly by distilling Red Cross prunes, apricots or raisins in contraptions made from Klim milk tins, which led to some hilarious evenings and terrible hangovers.

The compound had a theatre, which produced excellent shows and attractive leading 'ladies'. We had a nine hole golf course, on which we played with home made clubs and balls. There were soccer and hockey pitches, deck tennis and basket ball courts and a fire pool which was used by model yacht enthusiasts. In winter an area was flooded to form a frozen rink for skating and ice hockey. For our daily exercise we would walk round and round the perimeter of the camp, with German guards in their sentry towers looking down at us, which was known as bashing the circuit.

We had a weekly paper called *The Circuit*, and an ambitious monthly magazine called *The Spectator*. There was an exceptionally good library, with courses and lectures on almost any subject under the sun, and many prisoners managed to gain University Degrees while inside prison.

I had always been interested in natural history and wildlife, and grabbed the opportunity to read as many books as I could on the subject.

Like some conservationists, I was also keen on shooting and, to my shame, I had even sat up all night with a planter friend in North Malaya trying to shoot a tiger. We were deservedly almost bitten to death by mosquitoes in our rickety platform in the trees, and all we saw was a family

Making Booze in Stalag Luft III

of squealing wild pig which rushed out of the undergrowth obviously being chased by something. Our Malay guide said it could have been a tiger, but luckily for whatever it was it decided not to venture out into the open below us.

I had always felt a slight sense of guilt about shooting anything, but it wasn't until after the war that I gave up the habit for good. We were on a shooting trip at Bernin Kebbi in the far Northwest of Nigeria, and the local chief had provided us with flat-bottomed boats filled with straw in which to sit while waiting for the evening flight of geese and duck over the marshes. There was plenty of food and strong drink to fortify the spirit until the approach of dusk, and then all manner of wildfowl started flying over in their thousands. These were led by huge skeins of spur-winged geese and our guns started blazing away.

I don't know how many we shot but our African bearers kept plunging into the water to retrieve the dead and wounded birds. As they piled them into our boats I suddenly felt ashamed and tried to comfort myself with the thought that at least we could give them to some hospital somewhere to provide patients and staff with a feast. When I suggested this to my companions I was told that spur-winged geese were almost inedible and we were shooting them just for sport.

I have never raised a gun from that day to this, and I have become actively involved in various conservation bodies such as the Royal Society for the Protection of Birds and the World Wildlife Fund to make amends for a mis-spent youth.

I used to attend lectures on politics given by a very articulate Aidan Crawley. He was famous in the sporting world at home and he convinced many of us that it was only Christian to be a Socialist. After the war he became a Labour MP but when the Labour government was defeated he changed horses and became a Conservative, to the chagrin of all his converts.

I had always been brought up as a true blue Tory, but I began to have doubts after spending a training spell as a commercial traveller selling cigarettes in the Burnley,

Rochdale and Oldham area of the North of England during the depression of the 1930s. Most of the factories and cotton mills had been forced to close, and to see the soup kitchens, dole queues, and women wearing black shawls and wooden clogs, and children with runny noses and often no shoes at all, was enough to show me there was something terribly wrong with our society in those days.

Incredibly, the product I was selling in these depressed areas was one of the first brands of King Size cigarettes at a premium price. No one had any money but everyone was very friendly and polite although the stock phrase seemed to be " 'Ee, I'll not bother," whenever I plonked my brief-case down on the counter and started my selling spiel. When I asked my local supervisor what on earth one could say in reply, he said you merely say " 'Ee, but you must bother." This normally had the desired effect and I usually ended up with an order, but in smaller shops in the poorer districts I would tear these up because I knew the shopkeeper had no hope of selling the product in a thousand years.

Anyway, Aidan Crawley finally made up my mind for me, but it is infuriating to think that he ended up as a true blue Tory having converted me to a fairly bright shade of pink.

The Kriegies had their own gardens alongside their huts, with plenty of extra earth supplied from previous tunnelling, which provided vegetables and also flowers throughout the spring and summer months.

All this might sound rather like fun, but being a prisoner could be soul destroying. People who could occupy their minds and time came off best, and I occupied mine reading, attending lectures, bashing the circuit and producing the drawings for this book. The materials available for drawing were at first somewhat limited, until a Ferret saw me doing a caricature and asked me to do one of him for his family. I explained that I would need a mapping pen, indian ink, proper cartridge paper and coloured pencils to do the job properly, and from then onwards I had a regular supply.

There were only ten of us in our room, which included the secretive boffin Cundall, and Lou Barry who was a champion sculler, Cheese Lemon, a diminutive bomber pilot

Supplementing the Diet

covered in gongs, and Steve Stevens who spoke German fluently and was the unofficial camp interpreter. Steve had the Germans eating out of his hands and little did they know that his parents were German Jews.

We had Appell, or roll call, each day, taken by the German Commandant, with groups of German guards strutting around counting us as we paraded three deep in squads representing each hut.

There was the story that two prisoners had once escaped dressed as girls, having grown their hair long in camp and concealing it under their caps. Once outside the camp, they let down their hair and headed for the station to take a train towards France and freedom. They looked sufficiently presentable to attract the attention of two German soldiers in their compartment who soon discovered they were not female, although we were never told how. They were returned to the camp with their heads shaved and next morning, on Appell, the Camp Commandant ordered everyone to remove their head-dress. When the hair on several prisoners fell down to their shoulders, the culprits were marched sharply away to have their heads shaved and to spend a spell in solitary confinement.

Appell was often made a source of amusement for us in ways which would puzzle the Germans, who could never understand the British sense of humour. The camp's Senior British Officer was allowed to make announcements at the end of Appell before prisoners were dismissed. He would invariably say something ambiguous which would reduce us to peals of laughter. One method was to report the loss of books with invented titles and authors like 'Running Water' by I.P. Standing, which provided endless possibilities. There are numerous stories about the Germans being mystified by the British sense of humour, and we for our part, could find little subtlety in theirs.

Once, after the war, I had to entertain a group of Germans from our company's Hamburg factory who had won a trip to London as a reward for hard work and productivity. They had been told I had once been to Germany so they kept pressing me to tell them where I had been and what I thought of their fatherland. When I finally admitted that

106

I had only been there as a prisoner of war their spokesman beamed and said, "Ah, then you know how we suffered."

On another occasion, when we were trying to persuade the very teutonic boss of the same German company to help make our State Express 555 cigarettes international by introducing the brand on his market, he said this would be impossible because no German would ask for a brand called 'State Express, funf hundert, funf und funfzig'. We explained that consumers could be persuaded to call the brand 'drei funfen', like 'three fives' in Britain or 'tiga lima' in Malaysia, but the opportunity was lost because our teutonic friend had made his pronouncement and a retraction, in his German eyes, would have involved a loss of face.

Many people like myself, who have not had a University education, like to think that the best education in the world is in the so-called University of Life. If this is so then a large prisoner of war camp provides the best crash course imaginable. To live in close contact with all types and conditions of men confined behind barbed wire, often under conditions of stress and sometimes fear, is a unique education in human relations.

Natural leaders can appear among some of the mildest and humblest of men who set an example with their cheerfulness, endurance and courage under the most adverse conditions. On the other hand some perfectly normal and even tough looking people unexpectedly go to pieces, spending most of the day lying unshaven and dirty in their bunks, staring hopelessly at the ceiling or at the boards of the bunk overhead. The most tragic sight was to see some officers, when conditions got tough and food was really short, literally scraping the barrels which brought our food, using spoons or fingers to retrieve the last drop of liquid and scraps after our rations had been shared out among us. I met one of the most pathetic of these human scavengers after the war in Malaya. He held a senior government post and had a most attractive wife and family. He was bright, pleasant and cheerful, and I don't think he or anyone else sensed what I knew and I would have been the last to tell them.

At Sagan we were marched in small parties every two

weeks or so to have a communal shower in a large, white-tiled room in the main administrative building outside the prison's perimeter fence. There were numerous nozzles spaced throughout the room's ceiling and, although people claim that they knew nothing about the gas chambers in Nazi Germany, we must have known because we used to look apprehensively at the nozzles and heave a sigh of relief when they released nothing more sinister than powerful jets of warm water.

It was here that I learnt to appreciate the importance of dress, and uniforms with their insignias of rank, because there is nothing less impressive than a herd of naked men with the more elderly exposing their pot bellies and shrunken appendages. This is something even the Russians were quick to discover after the start of the war. Originally their officers and men wore more or less identical uniforms as befits the basic Communist belief, but this was soon changed until their officers started to look like Christmas trees with gaudy epaulets and masses of medals and metal decorations all over their chests.

However, I also learnt later that clothes alone do not always make the man or woman, when I took my Head Boy in Lagos to watch the Queen present Colours to the Nigerian Regiment. His name was Tom, and there was something suspicious because my cook and all the other house boys had told me their names were Thomas, Tom or Tommy when applying for a job, and I ended up with a complete household with names similar to my own. Anyway, on the way back from the Colour ceremony I asked Tom what he thought of our Queen. He replied very sadly that "She was no proper Queen because she never get big bottom." So clothes alone were obviously not the main yardstick for wealth and importance in Southern Nigeria.

When December came the war was in no way over, and the camp was covered in snow, with the temperature well below freezing. On the evening of the 24th, I asked the members of the original vetting committee if they would allow me to wear gym shoes and a balaclava helmet for my run round the camp next day. They readily agreed in view of the extreme cold, and early next morning the committee

108

and a few friends gave me an encouraging send off as I dashed out of the hut wearing nothing else but the blue ribbon.

I raced round the camp in a vain attempt to keep warm and cheated a bit by cutting corners. As I passed the sentry towers I heard the Germans clicking the safety catches on their rifles because they couldn't believe their eyes and suspected something suspicious must be afoot. I completed the circuit in record time and dashed back into the hut absolutely frozen, where my friends hurriedly wrapped me in blankets. I was so cold that when I looked down all I could see was the blue ribbon, because everything else had shrunk out of sight into my body. A Squadron Leader and journalist named Sidney-Smith gave me a wonderful sketch of this event, but unfortunately it was mislaid in the confusion when we were later evacuated from the camp ahead of the advancing Russians.

It seems incredible that with so many men confined in a camp with no female company there was no evidence as far as I could see of any active homosexuality. Perhaps the Germans put bromide in our food, which I am sure the RAF did in Habbaniya, and it was certainly true that our dreams in prison were more concerned with sugar, cream cakes and salt than with women. Even the most beautifully made up actors dressed as gorgeous girls in the camp plays seemed moderately safe, as I can vouch because I was often invited by Lou Barry to join them in celebration drinks after their performances.

I used to dream about English beer, Chinese noodles, Malay fried rice, and also the wonderful palm oil chops and groundnut stews of West Africa. Saturday and Sunday lunches in Nigeria were incredible affairs. They would start with cold beers and progress to 'coasters' which were pink gins with soda water and pearl onions which bobbed up and down on the bubbles. The origin of the soda water went back to the days when the local water was undrinkable, but it was such a pleasant drink it had remained immensely popular. The only problem was that lunch was always so late in coming that we had to survive on the pearl onions which meant drinking more and more 'coasters'. I introduced this drink to friends on my travels later through Latin

109

America, and I wonder if people like Charlie Gough still drink them in the Argentine and Southern Brazil where they became quite popular.

One Sunday lunch went on for so long I didn't return home until 6 o'clock although I was due to go out again at 8.30 for dinner. I asked my Steward boy, Philip, to wake me up at 7.30 which would give me just over an hour to sleep it off. When he called me I had a quick shower and put on my black tie and dinner jacket. I dashed down the steps to my car in the yard and met Kenneth Cooper who was the Manager of our company in Nigeria. I asked him in for a drink, explaining that I was a bit late for my dinner date. He gave me a frigid look, and told me to get out of my fancy dress and report to him immediately in his office. Our bachelor quarters were above the company office on the Marina in Lagos, and Philip had called me at 7.30 in the morning instead of 7.30 the night before.

Each hut at Sagan had at least one war map pinned on the walls which was kept up to date daily from information provided by the BBC or the Ferrets. By this time, the maps showed Sagan roughly half way between the Russian and Allied fronts. In January 1944 the Russians launched their huge offensive, swarming over the River Vistula and heading towards the Sagan area.

The Germans became increasingly nervous and edgy, and Steve told us they were planning to march us westwards ahead of the advancing Russians. We began to make haversacks out of any suitable material available which we packed with our few belongings. In my case these included the notes and illustrations for this book which I wrapped in greaseproof paper.

Our maps soon showed the Russians getting nearer and nearer, and on the evening of January 27th, when they had reached Breslau, only eighty miles away, we were told we must be ready that night for the march westwards. The ground was covered in snow and it was freezing cold, so we broke up chairs and furniture to make sledges, tied together with string, which we loaded with any Red Cross food available. Steve, in his capacity as camp interpreter, was able to visit the German Administrative block outside

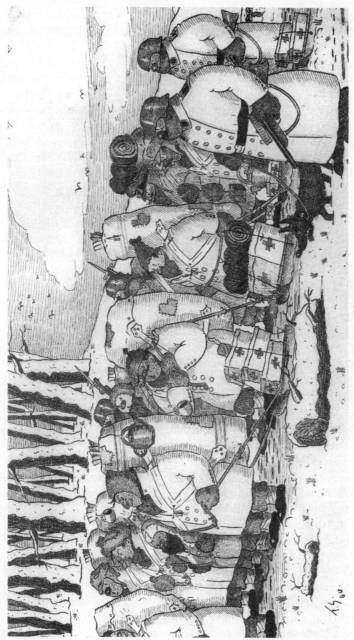

Going West

111

the camp where he managed to steal the German record cards of the two of us to provide a unique memento of our stay at Sagan.

The Germans kept delaying our departure, but just before dawn the next day we trooped out for the gruelling march along roads covered in snow and ice, escorted by German guards with tommy-guns and dogs. We marched for four days, averaging about twenty miles a day, and we had to wait in the freezing cold each night while the guards tried to find billets for our large numbers in village schools, churches and barns along the route. Only utter exhaustion made sleep possible in such conditions of extreme cold and discomfort.

We were continually being overtaken by long columns of refugees, fleeing from the Russians in horse-drawn wagons or on foot, with their belongings piled high in hand-carts of all descriptions. The icy roads and steep hills caused havoc among them with horses, wagons and carts sliding backwards, often ending up in the ditch, but on the third day of our march there was a thaw which melted the snow and ice.

This helped the refugees but it meant we had to discard our sledges and any Red Cross food which we couldn't carry. The refugees and local women, children and old men swooped on this discarded treasure which must have been a godsend to them at this difficult time. The Germans had been unable to feed us on the journey so it was now necessary to ration our remaining food carefully until we reached Spremberg late on the fourth day.

At Spremberg we were marched to the railway marshalling yard where we were given our first meal of the journey which was a bowl of hot, lumpy soup, known to us as Barley Goo. When we had finished our meal we were herded into cattle trucks, clearly marked '40 Hommes – 8 Chevaux', although the Germans managed to cram as many as fifty of us into each truck. We crouched or slept on a layer of straw covering the hard wooden floor, and there were no washing facilities or latrines except for one bucket placed in a corner of each truck. Many of the prisoners had dysentery or diarrhoea, which made the overnight journey to our destination, Luckenwalde, an uncomfortable and unpleasant

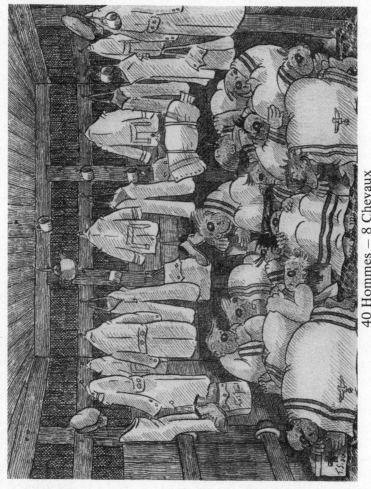

40 Hommes – 8 Chevaux

experience.

Luckenwalde was a dreary prison camp, thirty miles south of Berlin, which consisted of huge bare wooden huts crammed with bunk beds, three tiers high, to house four hundred and twenty officers in each hut. We slept on wooden boards and any available space was filled with wooden tables and benches, where we fed and spent the day.

The wash rooms were huge communal affairs and this was certainly true of the latrines, which consisted of rows of long wooden planks with holes every three feet or so and buckets underneath.

There were no longer any food parcels and our daily rations became more and more meagre as the Russians drew nearer. We were given two cups of mint tea or acorn coffee a day, a slice of dark dry bread with rancid margarine and at midday a bowl of Barley Goo, which sometimes contained a few lumps of horsemeat. Conditions were becoming desperate but we seemed to fare better than the poor Polish and Yugoslavian officers in neighbouring huts, and the only people who appeared better off were some Norwegians who were still receiving food parcels from their native country.

However, it was the Russian prisoners, brought into the camp to do all the filthy menial tasks, who suffered most and were being starved to death. The Germans would only give them enough food to keep them alive until the next batch of Russian prisoners arrived. Some of these starving Russian prisoners were in a terrible state with their ashen faces, sunken eyes and hollow cheeks. Their ragged uniforms bore large stencil marks branding them as Soviet prisoners to add to their humiliation. We sometimes managed to hand them food, cigarettes, or soap, but this usually infuriated their German guards who would promptly drive us away. The most tragic sight was to see some of these prisoners ravenously devouring the soap which made them foam at the mouth in front of our saddened eyes.

Those of us from room 14 in Sagan, had carried the bits and pieces of the secret radio with us, and it was now being assembled again each night to receive the BBC news. The camp was rife with rumours about Red Cross parcels being seen at the station, which always turned out to be false until a consignment did actually arrive one day which was shared out to give us half a parcel each.

By this time the Russians had overrun Sagan but had halted their offensive along the River Oder, after establishing bridgeheads on the Western bank, only sixty miles to the east of our camp. On March 23rd, it was the Western Allies turn to launch their new offensive, and they headed for the Rhine and crossed it. The excitement in the camp was unbearable as our radio mentioned names like Cologne, Kassel, Hanover, Magdeburg and Dessau, but then the Allies suddenly stopped at the River Elbe only thirty miles to our west. Berlin was hemmed in between these two huge invading armies and obviously only one of them would be given the honour of capturing the German capital.

It was to be the Russians, and on April 16th Zhukov's forces attacked along the Oder breaking through the German lines after three days fighting and then came racing towards Luckenwalde and Berlin. The Germans made an attempt to move us by rail down through the corridor to the south, where they said we would be held as hostages, but they were too late and the Russians too quick. The railway had been bombed almost to oblivion and most locomotives and wagons damaged beyond repair, so we were marched back to the relative safety of the camp.

One morning we were amazed to see the German guards and their officers fleeing the camp, which meant we were free to walk through the gates, except it was obviously safer to remain inside. We could hear gunfire all round us with German planes flying overhead one minute, and Russian Stormoviks and Yaks the next.

Soon after dawn the next day a great cheer went up, and we all rushed out of our huts to the barbed wire perimeter to see what was causing all the commotion, only to draw back in fear of our lives. The Russians in Stalin tanks were careering along the perimeter fence, tearing down the poles and the wire with German prisoners strapped to the front of the tanks. These poor Germans were green with fear as they were being hit and lacerated by the debris flying in all directions. Some tanks even had live pigs, sheep or calves strapped on the back, which the Russians had collected on the way for food, because their front line troops appeared to have no rations, and were expected to live off the land or on food captured from German troops. This horrifying episode was also included in the BBC 4's radio programme 'Prisoner of War'.

I suppose I had to try and understand the Russians, who had suffered so much when the Germans invaded their homeland, and who must have seen the terrible suffering of Russian prisoners of war. Also they hoped that the Germans strapped to their tanks would discourage the enemy from firing at them with anti-tank rockets and guns.

One or two tanks stopped near the shattered perimeter fence to allow the crews to rest and smoke a cigarette. They looked decidedly Mongolian and there were even some uniformed women among the crews. We tried to talk to them but they remained aloof, and had obviously been told not to fraternise with Westerners. The few Russian prisoners who were still alive were given arms by their liberators, and they headed out of the camp to the nearby town to cause havoc among the frightened German population.

Finally the Russian Infantry passed through en route for Berlin, consisting of rag-tag but disciplined columns of troops, carrying Russian and captured fire-arms. They were supported by a mixture of vehicles including some supplied from America, although all identification marks on these had been removed.

Then a very different type of Russian arrived, consisting of a contingent of smartly dressed soldiers, led by an officer covered in medals who was even smarter. They took over the control of the camp and we were virtually prisoners again, although we were allowed to go outside with armed Russian escorts on foraging parties to supply the camp with food. These Russians were always very correct but they remained aloof. At first their officer, with all his medals and gold epaulets, refused to believe we were officers because we wore simple battledress with only narrow cloth ribbons to show our rank.

The Russians treated the Norwegian officers with respect as they did some of the Yugoslav officers who presum-

Temporary Liberation

117

ably had fought with Tito and not with Mikajlovic. But God knows what befell the many Polish officers in the camp who were marched away and seemed to sense they were doomed.

When the Poles staged their famous uprising in Warsaw against the Germans as the Russians advanced against the city in the spring of 1943, Churchill was determined to drop them arms in parachute canisters, and we were standing by in 41 Squadron to escort our bombers back at the end of their long journey from Poland. When we heard the tragic news that the operation had been called off at the request of the Russians, who delayed their entry into the city to allow the Germans and Poles to annihilate each other, we knew, and every Pole knew, what fate the Russians had in store for the officers' class in Poland.

We couldn't understand why our Russian Allies continued to treat us as prisoners and when we heard they intended to repatriate us via far away Odessa, which was nonsense when the Americans were only thirty miles to the west, a radio message was transmitted asking for help. An American convoy arrived the next day and drew up outside our camp. We all rushed out with the minimum of belongings and jumped into the vehicles. One or two vehicles got away but the Russians, led by their officer, came running towards us firing over our heads and ordering us to disembark. After a heated argument between an American officer and the Russian, the convoy was forced to withdraw and we returned confused and sad to the camp.

The Russians had captured Berlin as long ago as May Day, the 1st of May, and VE day had come and gone on the 9th, but there was still no sign of our release. It wasn't until the 20th that the Russians decided to transport us to the Elbe themselves to be exchanged one for one with Russian prisoners liberated by the Western Allies. As we crossed a pontoon bridge over the River, the Russians asked us to wave and smile at their newsreel cameras to show our thanks, but we looked straight ahead and ran the last few yards to be greeted by grinning American GIs. Some of the freed Russian prisoners who were exchanged for us over the Elbe looked far from happy, and this incident, and the reasons why, are

118

mentioned in Count Nikolai Tolstoy's book, *The Victims of Yalta*.

The Americans took us by convoy to an aerodrome nearby, where they spoilt us with unlimited canned food, frozen drinks and hospitality. The US Air Force then flew us to Brussels where we spent a further two days in a Canadian barracks, which included one night out on the town which left us with terrible hangovers the next morning. Then the RAF flew us back to England where, like a Pope much later, we all kissed the ground as we stepped down from the aircraft.

I was home once again.

I immediately telephoned Mary's mother in Ayr to trace her daughter's whereabouts, only to be told she had just been married a few days previously. She had received no letters, the war in Europe had long been over, and everyone thought I was dead. So much for the sad forces of fate.

Soon afterwards the Japanese surrendered and global fighting ended. I applied for early demobilisation to take up Freddie Sargant's kind offer of my job back in the Far East, which wasn't such a bad life after all.

In War

In Peace

121

f

INDEX

123

126

128